GARDEN
ORNAMENT

SMITH & HAWKEN

GARDEN ORNAMENT

by Linda Joan Smith

WORKMAN PUBLISHING · NEW YORK

J. POTTSCHMIDT
5584 PALISADES DR.
CINTI., OH.   45238

Library of Congress Cataloging-in-Publication Data

Smith, Linda Joan.
Smith & Hawken Garden Ornament / by Linda Joan Smith.
p. cm.
Includes index.
ISBN 0-7611-1202-2
1. Garden ornaments and furniture. I. Smith & Hawken. II. Title.
SB473.5.S6 1998
717—dc21   97-44428 CIP

Workman Publishing Company, Inc.
708 Broadway
New York, NY 10003-9555

Manufactured by Arnoldo Mondadori, Verona, Italy

First printing February 1998
10 9 8 7 6 5 4 3 2 1

To those who have labored

through the centuries to create ornament of grace,

beauty, and imagination, and to the gardeners

who have taken it to heart.

CONTENTS

CHAPTER 4

EYE CATCHERS
AND SPACE MAKERS · 59

CHAPTER 5

WORKING ORNAMENT · 77

THE POWER OF ORNAMENT

Squat and utilitarian, but possessed of a simple beauty, terra-cotta rhubarb and sea kale forcers have a lengthy history in the English kitchen garden.

A ring dial, or armillary-sphere sundial (opposite), brings the mysteries of the heavens down to earth and into a garden courtyard.

THE DESIRE TO ADORN IS AS ancient as we are. To drape our necks with brilliant beads of shell or stone or to cloak our shoulders with flashing feathers. To paint figures upon the walls of our caves or to weave patterns in our baskets or cloth. To garnish our plates or to embellish our architecture. To set ourselves apart, establish our social standing, and enrich our bare surroundings.

"The first spiritual want of a barbarous man is Decoration," wrote philosopher Thomas Carlyle, and through the centuries humankind has proved him right.

Even in our gardens, bedecked with nature's finest fruits and flowers, the desire to ornament has been hard to resist. One gardener sets a cast-brass sundial at the heart of a bed of culinary herbs; another mounts a thatched-roof bird feeder atop a pole in a quiet, tree-lined corner of the yard. Still another places a pale marble figure in an alcove sculpted in a venerable hedge of yew,

A tepee of bamboo stakes supports a tangle of sweet peas, forming an ephemeral ornament as bright as spring. Once suited only for the kitchen plot, such makeshift structures lend grace to any country garden.

This staddle stone, mottled with lichen, once shouldered a heavy burden in the farmyard; now it brings an earthy weight to a carpet of campanula.

while a fourth nestles a mottled stone, carried from a nearby mountaintop, in a favored spot beside a mossy path. No matter the century in which they live or the land in which they dwell, all are placing their stamp upon their gardens and adding a human touch to nature's many glories.

We dress up and domesticate our gardens in other ways, of course: with fences, arbors, and furniture, along with pavings, walls, hedges, and imaginatively sheared shrubbery. Such features bring structure to a garden space and help define its mood and uses. But it is ornament that seasons the garden with mystery and subtle nuances of flavor, and ornament that makes us laugh or sets us to contemplation. Whether that ornament is fine art, folk art, or born of pure utility, whether it is steeped in tradition or has never been seen in a garden before, it delights the eye and makes the gardener's presence known.

Defining Garden Ornament

Graceful figures sculpted from marble or sumptuous urns carved from sturdy Portland stone have played a vital part in the history of garden ornament and readily spring to mind when the topic of garden ornament arises. But these formal garden works of art are far from ornament's only incarnation.

Ornament can be as simple as a terra-cotta pot, velvety with moss or marbled with a crust of salts, or as plain as a ceramic basin filled with water for the birds. A handful of shells, carried home from the beach and scattered in a flower bed, is ornament. So is a Victorian-era gazing globe, an old livestock-watering trough, a bamboo tepee smothered in scarlet runner beans, and a scruffy scarecrow standing guard in the corn patch.

Garden ornament also may find form as a ceramic plaque

mounted on a garden wall or fence, as a tiled fountain in a sunny courtyard, as a planter box painted with bold stripes of blue and white, or as a battered wooden wheelbarrow spilling a profusion of plants. You, the gardener, determine what is ornament and what is not; there are no absolutes, no rules that say you must choose the conventional over the quirky, or follow your neighbor's lead. Your garden is your own, and like your home, you may furnish it as you please.

The effective *use* of garden ornament, however, depends on more than whim and fancy. The same ornament that spoils one garden, dominating it like a bully or jarring it like a wrong note, may be just the spark that sets another garden ablaze. What distinguishes the two objects is their context: how each relates to the world around it.

Tradition is the language spoken by these antique urns, which stand like graceful sentries along a garden walk.

A marble maiden rests in a leafy bower (above); such finely sculpted statues have graced gardens for centuries.

A teardrop of stone, culled from a cider press and glazed by a trickle of water (left), beckons birds and butterflies.

Like a way station on a country road, this shapely birdbath gives the eye a place to rest as it gazes down a garden path, ensuring that an azure sea of irises cannot be overlooked.

Borrowed hardware from farmyard and lavatory come together in this flower garden (right) to promote an informal mood. A livestock watering trough or galvanized tub, filled to the brim and stocked with water lilies, also would support this garden's folksy tone.

Just as a deer emerging from the woods causes a hiker to slow and hush, this bronze stag (opposite) promotes stillness and contemplation in the garden.

Ornament's Power to Transform

Although it fulfills our primal desire for decoration, garden ornament—in proper context—becomes far more than the bric-a-brac on a mantel or the elaborate engraving on a silver tray. Gardeners who master ornament's use in regard to style, materials, scale, position, companion plantings, and historical and personal associations have power over nothing less than space, time, mood, and memory.

Well chosen and thoughtfully placed, ornament can transform our experience of the garden in the following ways.

Focus and space. Ornament brings focus to the garden and directs the eye of the onlooker just where the gardener wants it to go—much as a magician draws the glance of his audience with a gesture of the hand. Such ornament can expand or shrink the perceived size of the garden space, shape the path

one takes, influence where one pauses, and lure one's gaze away from the garden's flaws.

Time. Certain styles of ornament link the garden to the past, anchor it in the present, or nudge it toward the future. A classical-style urn or amphora, for instance, turns back the garden clock to a distant era, while an abstract sculpture fabricated from stainless steel advances it.

Location. Ornament crafted in an indigenous style or from local materials ties a garden to its native surroundings the way a saltbox house is wedded to New England and an adobe house is to Santa Fe. Other ornament, because of its borrowed style or materials, takes gardeners traveling: to Italy, England, France, Japan, and beyond.

The Magic of Meaning

Like poets who write between the lines, gardeners call on symbolic meaning to add depth and resonance to the garden. Some meaning we bestow ourselves; other meaning we inherit—from our families, from our churches, and from cultures around the world.

Employ the following ornament forms and motifs to enrich your garden's symbolic power.

Acorn. Life, fertility, and immortality

Cherub. Divine wisdom

Crane. Long life, vigilance, prosperity, happiness

Dog. Fidelity, watchfulness, a garden guardian

Doves. Love and constancy

Fruit. Abundance, autumn, the harvest

Lion. Strength, pride, courage, protection against evil, a guardian

Monkey. Man's folly

Pineapple. Fertility and hospitality

Sundial. The fleeting nature of time

Urn (with lid). Death and mourning

The size and weight of this boulder (above) makes it an ornament for the ages. Such permanent features serve as our legacy to the gardeners of the future.

Almost lost in the foliage, this low-lying birdbath (right) signals a gardener's love of wildlife and forms a counterpoint to leaf and blossom.

Large-scale ornaments such as a courtyard fountain bring welcome structure and a sense of stability to the garden.

Mood. Like sunlight or the sounds of trickling water, ornament works in tandem with the garden itself to alter the mood of all who enter: to provoke thought, induce calm, stimulate fantasy, promote laughter. And because many garden ornaments are easy to move around when inspiration strikes, the mood of the garden may be changed at will.

Structure and permanence. Large-scale garden ornaments, from sculpture and fountains to granite boulders and Venetian wellheads, help form the bones of the garden, giving it shape as well as a reassuring sense of permanence throughout the

Lavender-painted pots (above) play up the colors of kale and cabbage and coax the eye along a simple walkway. Their hue is irreverent—a far cry from traditional terra-cotta—but effective all the same.

seasons and as plants come and go. Such ornaments are the pillars upon which the garden is built, and part of the legacy a gardener leaves behind.

Seasoning. Ornament is the salt in the stew, the seasoning that brings out subtle garden flavors and melds disparate ingredients into a pleasing whole. Without it, even a masterfully planted and tended garden may seem vaguely unfinished, flat, and lacking in vitality.

Framing. Ornament enhances nature's beauty and strength, encouraging the garden visitor to see and appreciate

Like the spirit of stone incarnate, a woman's sculpted figure rises from a shapely boulder. Such nontraditional ornaments awaken emotions that a formal piece might not stir.

The obelisk, an ornament form as ancient as Egypt, punctuates country plots as well as formal gardens. This quirky pair, layered like cakes with native stone, stand guard over a gravel pathway.

A peasant spirit inhabits the stone form of a girl and her dog, standing serene in a cloud of 'Francine Austin' roses. The earthy carving seems more potent than the finely modeled figures of classical works and is ideally suited to the garden.

what might otherwise be missed. The tendril of a vine, for instance, may be lost in a sea of foliage until it reaches out and wraps around the gentle curve of a marble maiden's arm like a twining bracelet. And a thicket of ferns may be mere greenery until a fountain is secreted in its midst, and an oasis is born.

All these feats the right ornament, in the right garden context, performs with ease. But if ornament is chosen and placed only with the head, not with the heart, it remains merely a garden building block, adding to a garden composition that functions well but has no soul.

It is with an object's ability to please our senses and awaken our emotions that the full power of ornament takes root, matures, and finally flowers. A sculpture, fountain, whirligig, or cairn of rocks that we find beautiful or personally meaningful lends its grace to the trees and flowers around it, and instills a sense of depth and emotional resonance in the garden. Its form may please us the way paintings by Cezanne or Rembrandt delight lovers of art, because such works are powerfully composed or imaginatively seen. Its sound may soothe us as the wind sighing in the pines quiets the cares of a hiker in the wilderness. Its associations may awaken memories, the way smells reopen the doors to childhood. It may perfectly embody our personal ideal of beauty, forged upon the anvil of all we have seen and valued.

This is ornament at its full potential. It welcomes us into the garden, and makes us feel at home.

"Things are pretty, graceful, rich, elegant, handsome, but until they speak to the imagination, not yet beautiful."

—RALPH WALDO EMERSON, 1860

Anchors in a sea of foliage and flowers, a sundial and garden urn at opposite ends of a pathway tie the garden to the earth. They also serve as compass points in the garden's symmetrical layout.

BORROWED FROM THE PAST

WANDER THROUGH MANY a garden today and you can feel the touch of previous centuries. Hidden among the roses and the cedars are links to both the near and distant past: ornaments that have appeared, in one guise or another, in gardens throughout time.

A fountain, shooting forth vigorous jets or capturing water in a calming pool, ties us to the palatial gardens of the Sun King at Versailles as well as to Islamic gardens that sought to emulate Paradise as described in the Koran. A classical-style statue or urn leapfrogs us back through time to Victorian-era villa gardens, Italian Renaissance gardens, and all the way back to the gardens of ancient Rome itself. Even a simple clay pot connects us to the gardens of the past: tomb paintings depict their use in the time of the Egyptian pharaohs.

Rare, in fact, is the garden ornament that *doesn't* have historical precedent. "What has been done is what will be done; and

Walking stick in hand, this cultured gentleman is cast in lead, a material widely used in the eighteenth century. Many lead figures of the time were painted, but this one wears a natural patina.

Time stands still in this garden (opposite), which boasts many ornament forms from the past.

Wanted: Antique Ornament

Keep these tips in mind when you're on a quest for the perfect antique urn, statue, fountain, or finial.

Going up. Choose pieces that will hold or increase in value: items that are pleasing to the eye, finely crafted, in good condition, somewhat rare or unusual, and that have an attractive, natural patina. (To determine whether a piece is seldom seen or commonplace, do some detective work in books, auction catalogs, and stores or other retail sources.)

In shape. Antique ornament won't be pristine; most is far from it after years of exposure to the weather. But ideally, there should be no signs of major repair work, excessive restoration or cleaning, or

Stare at a sundial and the present slips away, replaced by a life in which the sun delineates the hours of the day and minutes pass at the pace of a shadow.

there is nothing new under the sun," wrote the author of Ecclesiastes a few centuries before the birth of Christ, and indeed, in the thousands of years ornamental gardens have been around, almost every form of ornament has come and gone and returned to grace the garden once again.

Such repeat performances haven't dulled ornament's appeal or jaded its audience. Instead, gardeners often choose ornaments specifically for their historical associations; such pieces bring a richness and depth to the garden that no new-fangled ornament can supply. Through them we experience not just the favored

extreme weathering or cracking (unless the damage adds to the piece's antique appeal).

Quality, not quantity. Buy the best you can afford. One fine lead cistern or carved stone urn can generate more atmosphere in the garden than four or five lesser examples, and will remain visually pleasing for many decades to come.

Buy what you love. Nothing is as important as this. No matter how esteemed it is by others, the finest nineteenth-century statue or Greek-style amphora will bring you little pleasure if it doesn't make you weak in the knees. Much better to buy the dented lead figure of Cupid to which you lost your heart, even though it dates from the 1920s and was once nearly as common in the garden as the sweet pea or morning glory.

ornament forms of the past, but the basic philosophies of garden making that first put them on the stage.

In the Beginning

Ever since the priests and rulers of ancient Egypt erected statues of their kings and deities in protected courtyards, ornament has played multiple garden roles, bringing artistry and spatial control as well as religious, philosophical, or intellectual content to the garden. But it is with ancient Greece and Rome—not Egypt—that the story of ornament in the Western garden truly begins.

That starting point is due not so much to the ancients' use of garden ornament (although the Romans did have majestic

This flower-filled basket finial (top), softened by the years, lends a sense of history and domesticity to a rose-covered garden wall.

*F*igures of Diana, the huntress, bring classical power to the garden.

*I*nspired by classical works, statues of chubby children known as "putti" (above) have charmed garden visitors since Renaissance times.

*I*talian gardens blossomed with elaborate fountains during the Renaissance.

ornamental gardens dominated by architecture and statuary), but to their ability to inspire the use and design of garden ornament all the way to the present day.

At no time was this as true as during the Italian Renaissance. Particularly during the sixteenth century, wealthy princes and patrons of the arts built extensive terraced gardens based upon the models of the classical age, through which they explored man's relationship to nature and the joining of nature and art.

The gardens' controlled geometric designs reflected their owners' belief in a cosmic order. Their plantings expressed an appreciation of nature and a desire to know and master her myriad wonders. Their elaborate fountains celebrated both the hydraulic achievements of the classical world and the life-giving forces of the natural one. Their man-made grottoes, complete with water surprises (which soaked unwary visitors) indicated a love of

humor as well as a passion for nature untamed. And their ornament, whether excavated from ancient sites or newly made, provided an allegorical pathway to a rich body of mythological themes and meanings.

Here were allusions to Mount Parnassus, the Garden of the Hesperides, and bucolic Arcadia, where Pan roamed amid the water nymphs and river gods. Here were Pegasus and Apollo, Cupid and Venus, Hercules and Antaeus, and sphinxes and fauns, along with assorted dragons, unicorns, swans, turtles, and lions. Here too were shepherds and shepherdesses, and innumerable fat putti. All had symbolic meaning easily understood by the sixteenth-century garden visitor well versed in classical themes.

Like all classically inspired ornament, figures of fleet-footed Mercury alluded to powers not immediately apparent. This youthful figure, carrying a caduceus, represented the communication between heaven and earth; through Mercury, the will of the gods was made known.

"*These figures represent all the several deities, and illustrious persons of antiquity, which should be placed properly in gardens, setting the river gods, as the* Naiades, Rivers, *and* Tritons, *in the middle of fountains and basons; and those of the woods, as* Sylvanes, Faunes, *and* Dryads, *in the groves.*"

—A. J. DÉZALLIER D'ARGENVILLE, *THE THEORY AND PRACTICE OF GARDENING*, 1712

THE MEASURE *of* TIME

It's an odd bit of irony. Place a sundial properly in the garden and it marks the passage of time. Yet that same sundial brings a sense of timelessness to the garden that few other ornaments can match. Its dial invites us to linger, while the sun shines and a telling shadow creeps like night across its face. Its motto invites us to ponder the way we pass our hours. And its design, an ancient marriage of science and art, invites us to consider—from our little patch of earth—the movement of the heavenly spheres.

Small in size, it measures mighty things. "A Dial is the Visible Map of Time," wrote Robert Hegge in 1630, ". . . the Anatomie of the Day and a Scale of Miles for the Jornie of the Sun."

Sundials have been in use in one form or another since humans first noted the sweep of shadows across the land, but it wasn't until the sixteenth century that they were widely made. Hundreds of sundial designs have graced gardens since that time, from vertical dials mounted on walls or the sides of homes and churches to ring dials based on the form of the armillary sphere—an ancient astronomical instrument based on the Aristotelian and Ptolemaic view of the universe.

In that view (since eclipsed by Copernican theory), the earth was at the center of a sphere of fixed stars that rotated completely every 24 hours. Likewise, the sun, moon, and planets also were fixed on transparent spheres, each with the earth at its center. An armillary sphere modeled this cosmic system of nested spheres.

Armillary-sphere sundials are simpler than true armillary spheres; their metal rings rep-

The gnomon's shadow on the dial face indicates the time.

On this dial, a taut wire casts the time-telling shadow.

A tangle of clematis obscures the time but fosters beauty.

resent only the outer sphere of fixed stars. The primary ring on an armillary dial is the equatorial band, a projection of the earth's equator onto the celestial sphere. Rings set at right angles to the equatorial band usually represent the solstitial and equinoctial colures. A fourth ring, set at an angle to the equatorial ring, usually is the ecliptic band that represents the apparent path of the sun around the earth. An arrow through the sphere's center corresponds to the earth's axis; the shadow it casts upon the inner surface of the equatorial band (which is marked with hour lines) displays the time.

Simpler to understand, and beloved through the centuries, is the horizontal or flat sundial, set on a pedestal in a sunny clearing. Often made of stone or metal, a flat dial looks like a lopsided clock face (with an arc rather than a circle of numbers) and frequently bears a thought-provoking motto. Fixed upon it like a sail is a gnomon (usually made of metal), which casts the time-telling shadow across the dial's face. The gnomon's angled upper edge is called the style.

For greatest accuracy, a flat dial must be designed and situated to reflect a garden's physical location on the sphere

A fluted baluster elevates this antique dial.

The angle of the gnomon must correspond to local latitude.

An armillary-sphere dial also uses a shadow to tell time.

Sundial Mottoes

Come Light! Visit Me!

*Light and Shadow by Turns
But Always Love*

---

*Let Others Tell of
Storms and Showers
I'll Only Count Your Sunny Hours*

---

*Light Rules Me
The Shadow, Thee*

The Shadow Passes; Light Remains

---

*Life's But a Shadow
Man's But Dust
This Diall Says
Dy All We Must*

This equatorial dial is a simplified armillary-sphere dial.

of the earth. If a garden is located in San Francisco, for instance, between latitudes 37 and 38 degrees north, the angle between the style and the horizontal plane of the dial's face should be approximately 37.5 degrees (get out your protractor). A sundial calibrated for San Francisco will *not* work as well in either San Antonio or Minneapolis. To correct this, shim the face of the dial up on one side or the other until the style makes an angle with the horizon equal to the local latitude.

In addition, the gnomon, which lines up with the numeral twelve (noon), must point toward the geographic north pole (denoted by the north star, not by a compass). If you live in the southern hemisphere, the gnomon must point to the south pole. To locate the geographic poles, draw a few concentric circles on level ground in a sunny spot, and place a dowel upright at the circles' exact center. Make sure the dowel is vertical. In the morning, when the tip of the dowel's shadow just touches one of the circles on one side, mark that point. In the afternoon, when the tip of shadow touches the same circle on the opposite side, mark that point. Draw a line between the two points; then draw

another line that bisects the first line at right angles. The second line points north and south.

Even when your dial is properly oriented, don't expect to set your watch by it—unless it's also marked with the equation of time. Our rigid clocks measure out mean solar time, while sundials indicate apparent solar time. The two match up exactly on only four days of the year: April 15, June 15, September 1, and December 24 (not counting the complication of daylight savings time). The equation of time helps sundial owners calculate the difference between clock and sundial time, which can come in handy if you're up to your elbows in compost but have other appointments to keep.

For more information on sundials, contact the North American Sundial Society, 8 Sachem Drive, Glastonbury, CT 06033; (860) 633-8655. A useful website is Sundials on the Internet: http://www.sun-dials.co.uk. For advice on the history, acquisition, or care of antique sundials and scientific instruments, or help with identification, contact Sara Schechner Genuth at Gnomon Research (Customized Curatorial Services), 1142 Loxford Terrace, Silver Spring, MD 20901; (301) 593-2626.

Dials with built-in basins double as birdbaths.

Dials are best located in a central, sunny garden spot.

This complex armillary-sphere dial tells more than the time.

A fluted column raises a dial above a sea of 'Grosso' lavender.

A classic armillary-sphere dial needs no embellishment.

This equatorial dial is simplified to its essence.

The wide, flat ring on this dial is the equatorial band.

Vertical dials must be mounted so they face south.

This square baluster complements the dial it supports.

Simple dials and supports are well suited to small spaces.

A weighty base counterbalances a large armillary-sphere dial.

A butterfly tells time on this geometric dial.

A noble maiden reigns over a shaded garden corner; she's set on a pedestal for better viewing from afar.

Another stately figure peers from a leafy bower; her missing forearm and heavily draped garment add to her aura of antiquity.

Art Versus Nature

The well-ordered and ornamented gardens that spilled down the hillsides of central Italy spawned imitators throughout Europe, particularly in France. But whereas art and nature had achieved a dynamic balance in Italy's gardens, in the gardens of seventeenth-century France, art was clearly king. France's relatively flat terrain allowed the geometric ideal—a garden with a strong central axis crossed at right angles by other axes—to shine. In fact, in the garden of Louis XIV at Versailles, such geometry obliterated the natural landscape as far as the eye could see, symbolizing not only man's control over nature, but the king's power over his subjects. The countless statues and ornaments in servitude throughout the garden deepened this theme; their allegorical link was Apollo, god of the sun, with whom Louis had been identified since birth.

Such extreme order and artificiality invited a stylistic backlash during the following century. Inspired in part by landscape paintings of classical Arcadia, Englishmen such as William Kent and Lancelot "Capability" Brown brought nature back to the garden, often romanticized in the form of pastoral parklands where grazing sheep, Palladian pavilions, and streamside nymphs were the primary ornament. It was a style much imitated by the landed elite on the continent as well as in the fledgling United States.

Banished were formal parterres edged in clipped box, baroque fountains dripping with decoration, and regiments of marble statues, replaced instead with serpentine paths through shaded vales, cascading streams, and mist-shrouded views of classical temples through carefully placed clumps of elm and chestnut. Also favored were lead statues representing the pastoral way of life, such as gamekeepers, haymakers, mowers, shepherds, and shepherdesses, often painted in true-to-life hues.

Only the richest landowners could afford such costly theatricality and devote so much land to nonproductive uses, whether in the Italian-, French-, or English-landscape style, or assorted offshoots. Poorer folk, if they had any land at all, tended plots devoted exclusively to growing turnips and potatoes, native flowers, and herbal medicines for their families; fancy statuary would have been as unthinkable among their columbines and cauliflower as Wedgwood china on their tables.

A Garden Revolution

In the nineteenth century, however, a new type of garden owner surfaced, buoyed by spoils of the Industrial Revolution. These merchants and mill owners were members of the emerging Victorian middle class and strove to gain a social foothold by imitating the formal parterres and urn-dotted allées they associated with wealth. To them, ornament equaled status: a stepping-stone to a life of grace and privilege.

They bought up cast-stone statues and cast-iron urns and fountains by the score, mass-produced by new manufacturing methods. They set them amid parterres filled with exotic new bedding plants pinched to a uniform height, and relished the often gaudy effect. Though there was also a vogue for rustic adornment, the classically inspired gardens of the Italian Renaissance were the primary source for Victorian ornament and geometry; travelers on the Grand Tour had seen their wonders firsthand. Unlike the Italian models, however, Victorian gardens often were formulaic, executed without regard for surrounding terrain, architecture, and native plant life or climate. Absent,

Statues of Pan were favored during the Renaissance as well as during England's pastoral landscape period. As god of the fields, pastures, and herds, Pan was ideally suited to the garden.

Antique statues stand out best against a simple backdrop, such as a clipped hedge of yew. This dapper gentleman loiters in a green alcove in a vast wall of shrubbery.

*"Too often, however, the
return to formalism
about the house was
accompanied by the
advent of hideous cement
vases filled with lobelia
and geraniums. In mod-
ern times gardeners have
found more pleasing
substitutes, such as terra-
cotta vases and oil jars."*

—GERTRUDE JEKYLL,
  GARDEN ORNAMENT, 1918

*This aged stone urn has stood
for decades at the center of the
garden while countless flowers
have come and gone. Such
ornaments seem as rooted to
the soil as the oldest of trees.*

too, was the underlying allegory that gave the Italian statuary meaning and purpose. Instead, pure decoration prevailed.

But the pendulum was swinging. And this time, inspiration was as close as the cottage down the road.

Back to Basics

The tyranny of the Italian or French style—enforced by clippers, mowers, and a legion of opinionated garden writers—did not exist in the lowly cottage garden. Instead, roses tumbled over rustic fences, seducing passersby with their heady scent. Pinks and poppies fraternized along well-trodden pathways. Irises and lilies

A massive earthenware jar (left) remains empty at the heart of this box-edged garden, a fitting repository for the spirit of the past.

A soot-blackened chimney pot (below), transformed into a planter, occupies a central garden spot.

Centuries-old lead cisterns became coveted ornaments during the early 1900s; today, gardeners seek fine reproductions of the form.

raised their colorful heads above the cowslips and columbines, and parsley and cabbage mingled with the chamomile. The only ornament was born of utility: a spiraled bee skep raised on a footstool to outwit the mice, a basin of water for the resident cat, a simple wooden bench beneath the shade of a heavy-laden apple.

Here was life, uncontrived and unpretentious. Compared to the starched, formal gardens of the well-to-do, it looked like heaven, at least to late-century English gardeners and writers William Robinson and Gertrude Jekyll.

Between them they would bring art and nature back into balance, and affect the course of garden design to the present day. Their advice led to long-blooming gardens that were glorious hybrids, still containing structure (often in the form of screening hedges that divided the garden into discrete sections), but softened by masses of hardy flowering perennials and cottage-

GARDEN STANDING STONES

They look like giant mushrooms spawned at Stonehenge: mysterious pairs of rocks, piled one on top of the other in the perfect shape of a prized *champignon*. Unlike England's mysterious standing stones, however, their origins are easily explained.

The staddle stone's mushroom shape has practical roots.

Known as staddle stones, or rick stones, these odd constructions were used for centuries by England's farmers to raise granaries, tithe barns, or rick settles up off the damp ground and protect the year's harvest from ravenous rats and mice. Critters could scurry up the rough stems of a granary's staddle stones, but couldn't negotiate the vertical overhangs of their mushroom-shaped caps.

Led by the likes of Gertrude Jekyll, turn-of-the-century gardeners recycled these once-common relics as rustic pedestals for sundials or small statues. Today, authentic staddle stones are in great demand as garden sculpture in both England and the United States, and need no further embellishment. Standing thigh high in the perennial bed or woodland garden, or better yet, among the bush beans and sprawling squash, they recall an agrarian life fast disappearing from the landscape. (Cast-stone reproductions also are available.)

Gardeners without access to these agricultural relics need not do without their charm. To stack up your own rustic staddle stone, seek out a suitable upright stone for a base at a quarry or landscape materials yard. Cut-stone blocks known as ashlar may work best. (Look in the Yellow Pages under Landscaping Supplies, Quarries, Rock, or Stone.) Then choose a second stone that will balance on top of the base. Putting the two together won't be much different from piling rocks into a cairn along a mountain trail.

Most suppliers will deliver and situate your rocks for a fee. Provide a firm foundation, or sink the base of the bottom rock into the soil to ensure stability.

This stone's cap is lost in a cloud of blooms.

Staddle stones draw the line between field and lawn.

garden plants, native trees, and unclipped shrubbery.

Although herbaceous plants were the focus, such gardens often included traditional ornament, from oversized terra-cotta oil jars and sundials on stands to stone benches or lead statues. Other ornament types were borrowed from town, house, and farm, including lead cisterns, marble bathtubs, stone sinks, stone watering troughs, sarcophagi, and wellheads (used as planters), along with millstones, stone lawn rollers, chimney pots, and staddle stones (employed as bases for sundials or statuary). All brought a feeling of warmth and domesticity to the garden that has rarely been surpassed.

Bringing It Home

Today, an interest in antique ornament forms has blossomed as gardeners cultivate a sense of romance and permanence in their herb gardens, perennial borders, or box-edged flower beds. There is no quicker route to making a young garden feel established than the inclusion of old ornament.

A massive millstone fills a clearing in a wooded glen. Smaller millstones often are found in gardens, serving as the bases for sundial pillars, as foundations for statuary, or as oversized stepping-stones.

Vintage four-season figures can still be found occasionally at garden statuary auctions and antique stores specializing in garden ornament. Newer versions are still being made today and are readily available.

Advancing Antiquity

Waiting is part of a gardener's territory: the anticipation of harvesting the garden's glory is almost as sweet as the taste of the fruit. But when it comes to waiting for ornament to weather, we're as impatient as kids on a cross-country car trip. "Are we there yet?" is never far from the tip of our tongue.

Eventually, time, water, and the changes of the seasons *will* do their work, encouraging the growth of moss, lichen, and the staining and weathering that signal age. But there are ways to hurry the process along.

Encourage the growth of moss or lichen on terra-cotta, stone, wood, or cast-stone ornaments by the following method. Wet the pot or ornament well (if possible, soak it overnight). Brush with a mix of one part active-culture plain yogurt and two parts water; alternately, use beer, butter-milk, sour milk, or manure

Classical putti frolic with barnyard pigs (top).

Garden boutiques specializing in antique ornament now grace most major cities, where those with deep pockets can buy up antique armillary-sphere dials, sundials, statues, urns, fountains, cisterns, birdbaths, and pots, along with architectural pieces such as pedestals, capitals, and columns. Most date from the late nineteenth and early twentieth centuries, although some older pieces occasionally are available. Antique stores, architectural salvage companies, and auctions also are good places to hunt for treasures, and the sharp-eyed garage-sale or flea-market shopper may even have some luck.

Determining the age and authenticity of a piece can be difficult. Modern reproductions are increasingly plentiful, and many old garden ornaments that survive today are themselves reproductions of earlier examples and may be passed off as older than they are. Patina is of little help in determining age; many garden ornaments rapidly gain a convincing surface when exposed to even a few years of water, dirt, and weather, or they can be artificially or chemically aged.

Barring years of comparative study, the safest route when buying antique garden ornament is to work with an established dealer and to ask for a written guarantee that the piece is as it is represented. Most reputable dealers are willing to supply one, allowing the piece to be returned if any questions arise.

Once your garden prize is safe at home, be sure to keep it out of harm's way. First and foremost, resist the temptation to share its glory with the neighborhood. Although it may seem selfish, it's best to keep antique ornament in a section of your garden that can't be seen from the street; as old ornament rises in value, it is increasingly the target of thieves. And don't think weight is an automatic deterrent. Fountains and bronze statues weighing hundreds of pounds have been known to disappear overnight.

tea. Keep the object moist and in the shade. Repeat the procedure if necessary. If you already have moss growing in your garden, rub a clump over the surface of the ornament to inoculate it with spores. Or puree moss and one of the liquids above in a blender, and apply this potion to the ornament.

If a change in surface color is what you're after (and the ornament in question is not of great value), experiment with surface applications of penetrating stain or diluted paint, rubbed on with a cloth or applied with a brush and rubbed off with a cloth. Wet coffee grounds, tea leaves, and manure will also stain many surfaces. Or if the ornament is easy to move about, you can speed up the aging process by burying it in damp earth or leaving it in tall grass or a dense thicket of plants for a few months. Otherwise, cultivate patience. Nature works wonders in her own sweet time.

Replicas of antique statuary mix with urns and jars.

*H*and-thrown flower pots and Long Toms (tall pots for growing tap-rooted plants or plants with deep root systems) await buyers at a traditional European pottery (right).

*M*assive jars accented with high-relief grapes and vining leaves (below) have a mellow antiqued finish.

*H*ares and hounds join an eclectic array of newly made ornament at this sales yard.

Give your piece of history a stable foundation of ample size, and place it where it won't be knocked into by romping kids, dogs, or overactive party guests. In earthquake country, keep top-heavy statues set low to the ground and away from garden seating areas. In cold-weather climes, you may need to give antique ornament winter protection to avoid frost and salt damage (see "Weathering All Storms," page 98).

Grand Impersonators

A single antique urn, set atop a low brick wall and mottled with lichen, can transform the garden's character. But so can a reproduction of an antique piece, at far less cost and with much less worry about breakage or theft. Garden shops, nurseries, and mail-order sources offer an increasing array of garden ornament made in an antique style, from Italian terra-cotta pots and Roman-style lead troughs to cast-stone fountains, finials, and a wide array of statuary.

Some ornaments have been given a weathered look with stains, paint, or other treatments; others will quickly acquire a pleasing patina in the garden. All have the potential to become heirlooms in their own right as the years pass.

If possible, shop around before you buy, comparing prices, designs, and quality of craftsmanship. Look for pieces with simple, classic lines and decorative molding or sculpting that is well defined. Avoid pieces that are awkwardly proportioned, sloppily made, or overly ornate no matter how well priced; they will detract from your garden's natural beauty rather than enhance it.

"The fountains . . . may be procured, at very reasonable prices, in artificial stone, of Mr. Austin, New Road, London; and also in iron, of Mr. Rowley, Howland Street, Fitzroy Square, and others."

—CHARLES MCINTOSH,
*THE NEW AND IMPROVED
PRACTICAL GARDENER*, 1839

Frogs, fish, and waterfowl cavort in this retail oasis, tempting visitors to take them home. Such figures will bring the soothing sounds of trickling water to even the plainest pond.

A SENSE OF PLACE

BEHIND EACH GARDEN GATE LIES a new world, unexplored and unknown. Yet step through the portal and you will find familiar landmarks. Like the obelisk that marks our nation's capital, or London's tower of Big Ben, these distinctive garden objects let you know exactly where you are and what you can expect.

Such ornament is a sort of sign language. Without a word being said, it can set a tone, establish a style, and reveal the garden's geographic and cultural roots.

Much of that happens naturally and without undue thought. Geographic proximity, for instance, makes more Mexican ornaments available (and affordable) in the Southwest, while more classical statuary, made by long-established New England firms, turns up in the gardens of East Coast states.

Yet it's also possible to choose garden ornaments with a conscious goal in mind, becoming fluent in their language and using them intentionally to strengthen your garden's sense of place.

This dignified figure would seem as misplaced as a coyote among the lush gardens of the East or South, but it resonates with meaning in a New Mexico courtyard.

Gardens in arid lands have long relied on fountains for their oasislike nature. This terra-cotta-colored cement fountain (opposite) blends well with the native sandstone of the surrounding landscape.

The Lay of the Land

An eagle on the wing flies where raptors soar and dive, and suits the rugged nature of the Southwestern hills.

The most elemental garden landmarks tell us physically where we are. They arise from the local geography, reflect the climate, and echo the natural landscape. They tie the garden to the land the way our habits tie us to our upbringing. The origin of each element is clear; its form and substance makes a satisfying sort of sense.

The great waterworks of Italian Renaissance gardens, for instance, are inseparable from the tumbled hillsides around Rome, and the attendant marble statues seem to have sprung full-grown from the marble-laden earth. Beneath the Italian sun their crystalline flesh is haloed with light.

Traditional Japanese garden ornament, likewise, is wedded to the native terrain; each rock or pool or sweep of gravel distills the

A fat earthenware jar (above) is equally at home in Spain, the sunny south of France, or the arid hills of California.

England's soft hills and sweeps of green (right) call for ornaments of native stone, such as this sundial pillar and path.

Carefully composed native stones form a waterfall that rivals nature's beauty in this Japanese-style garden.

The rugged mountains of Japan's island landscape are echoed in miniature in the cascading rocks of a garden (below).

Nature's imperfections are honored in the offset stones of a garden path.

beauty of the country's mountains and waterfalls into miniature or symbolic form. Even nature's imperfections and asymmetry are paid homage in the meandering of a course of stepping-stones or the intentional chip on a water basin's rim.

Such ornament seems part of the land, as if it grew up from the soil along with the cedars or the maples. Try to move it, and you'd expect to find roots reaching deep into the earth.

Establishing this organic sense of strength can be as simple as choosing ornament made from materials that are naturally part of the garden, such as wood, stone, and earth (in the form of terra-cotta or other pottery). After years in the garden, ornament made from these materials weathers to a fine silver or attracts mosses

Sandstone from the Southwest looks best in its home environment. Here, sandstone slabs fan out from a garden bell tower; the gaps between the stones provide a toehold for lavender-blossomed thyme.

The jagged form of this local slate brings a different feeling to the garden than would a smooth granite boulder or chunk of volcanic tuff.

and lichens that magnify the beauty of the surrounding plants, whether rock rose, peony, or lilac.

Native stone, in particular, helps establish a sense of place. Before the coming of the railroads, rock rarely strayed far from its quarry of origin; now, native stone continues to be most effective when used in gardens close to home. Older gardens on California's Monterey Peninsula, for example, have pathways or planting beds made from Carmel stone, a locally quarried sandstone now in short supply. Its soft, sandy nature and light colors in swirls of cream and ocher set off the area's somber cypress and bring warmth to the garden when the ocean fog rolls in, far more effectively than stone imported from even a hundred miles away. In the same way, the bluestone of Pennsylvania, sandstone of the Southwest, limestone of the Midwest, and fieldstone of Vermont all establish a garden's geographic—and geologic—identity. Each is naturally well suited to weather local storms and provide a pleasing foil for native plant life. More than that, such stone says to all who see it: these are gardens that are of this place.

Other ornament can just as easily set the scene. A piece of driftwood dragged home from a nearby beach or a fallen log salvaged from the nearby woods will tie your garden to its surroundings, as will an urn thrown from local clay by a local potter, or stepping-stones embedded with pebbles sieved from your garden's beds. Look at the landscape around you, and let its forms and nature guide you.

Stacked fieldstone borders many a New England garden and pasture; building a wall was the easiest thing to do with the stones as they were cleared from the fields.

A carved ram's head (above) brings ancient Aztec or Incan civilizations to mind and blends well with other Southwestern imagery.

This desert garden blossoms with fragile earthenware jars, which look like prized archaeological finds left by long-vanished people.

A MATTER *of* SUBSTANCE: MATERIALS *for* ORNAMENT

The material a garden ornament is made from shapes its character over time. Stone, cast stone, ceramic, wood, and a variety of metals all have proved their worth through centuries, lending their innate strength, weight, and sense of permanence to flower bed and greensward alike. True, clever imitations for traditional materials exist and are easy on both the wallet and the back (who wants to shift a real bronze statue even an inch to the right or left?). But there's not a resin or plastic around that can match the cool allure of genuine Carrara marble, or equal terra-cotta's sun-baked warmth.

*S*tone lions guard a garden pathway, their fierceness softened by age.

Here's a gathering of time-tested materials revered by gardeners past and present.

Marble. Marble's luster has attracted the sculptor's chisel since the days of the ancient Greeks; such crystallized limestone was one of the earliest materials used for outdoor ornament and continues to evoke the classical age.

Although, in general, the skill with which marble is worked has slipped severely during the twentieth century, all marble statues continue to be individually sculpted, making each ornament slightly different from the next. Even replicas of classical statues, such as the *Venus de Milo* or the *Apollo Belvedere,* vary in detail and proportion from one example to another.

Limestone. Warmer in tone than marble, and without marble's polish, limestone is at home in cool or foggy climes. Formed from the remains of sea shells and other organic materials, limestone is relatively easy to carve. And the more porous the limestone type, the more readily the ornament will welcome the growth of mosses and lichens, adding a sense of antiquity to the garden even when quite new.

Many ornaments made in Italy during the twentieth century are of Vicenza limestone, a particularly porous, easy-to-carve stone. In England, Portland stone (a hard limestone type) was widely used for carving pedestals, vases, urns, and statuary during the eighteenth and nineteenth centuries; antique Portland stone ornaments are eagerly sought by collectors.

Cast stone. Cast stone began to stand in for real stone in the mid-eighteenth century; ornament made from it could be molded rather than carved, and was therefore cheaper than real stone ornament to produce. Formulas for cast stone varied but were either clay-based (and fired for durability) or cement-based. So high was the quality of pieces produced in the eighteenth and nineteenth centuries that they are often mistaken for real limestone. Some can be identified by their lack of natural veining or deposits, by air pockets on their surfaces, or by aggregate exposed in breaks or cracks. High-quality cast-stone ornaments from the nineteenth century and earlier often remain, today, as sharp in detail as when they were made.

Today's cast-stone statues, stepping-stones, fountains, and birdbaths are largely cement-based; good pieces have a natural, stonelike finish and

Marble gleams against a backdrop of greenery, whether in the form of a garden sylph, a Venetian wellhead, or a basin for the birds.

Limestone is well suited for garden plinths and pillars.

Over time, some cast stone reveals its aggregate.

*H*and-thrown English terra-cotta has a timeless allure.

*T*hese molded terra-cotta planters from Italy bear foliate designs.

*S*toneware jars and basins conjure up the Far East.

color, with no exposed aggregate, and are finished by hand to remove flaws left by the molding process.

Some of the finest cast-stone ornament is made in England, both by Chilstone and by Haddonstone, Ltd. These ornaments look like carved limestone or sandstone, and replicate hard-to-find antique pieces such as sundial pillars, fountains, and obelisks. They are available in the U.S.

Terra-cotta. The most familiar form of terra-cotta to gardeners is the simple earthenware garden pot, made from fired red clay. Terra-cotta pots were thrown by hand on a potter's wheel from ancient times until the mid to late nineteenth century, when mechanized pot-making was widely adopted; now, some pots are once again being fashioned by hand. No matter the method of their making, terra-cotta pots, cloaked in moss and overflowing with flowers, make a garden seem like home.

Stoneware. Most stoneware ornament unearthed in today's gardens consists of colorful glazed urns, pots, oil jars, and fishbowls imported from China, Malaysia, Thailand, and other Far Eastern countries. High heat gives stoneware its superior strength, causing the clay to vitrify during firing.

Bronze. Ornaments cast from this copper alloy are among the garden's finest, both sharp in detail and striking in color. Bronzes often wear a chemically induced patina ranging in color from red-brown to green or gold; if left exposed to the weather, the applied patination eventually will be replaced by a streaked finish of turquoise green, white, and black.

Although extremely durable (hence their popularity for commemorative statues in public parks), bronze casts have always been costly to make. As a result, ornament manufacturers through the years have offered up an array of impostors—from terra-cotta to zinc—coated or electroplated with a bronzelike finish.

Lead. Early lead statues had many of the same attributes as those of costly bronze: more than one statue could be cast from a mold, they were immune to frost, and they were inhospitable to lichen. Figure in their low cost (lead was easier to cast and finish than bronze), and it's clear why they reigned in English gardens throughout the eighteenth century.

Lead is both extremely heavy and brittle, so the extended appendages on antique lead figures have often been broken, and statues and urns have sometimes slumped from the weight of the material alone. Newer lead figures are less prone to such structural problems.

Iron. Cast iron was a particularly popular material for urns, vases, and fountains during the nineteenth century. Cast iron is stronger than lead, but it may break if struck or dropped, is difficult to repair, and will readily rust.

Many modern ornaments are made from steel that develops an intentional patina of rust as it ages.

Wood. In some cases, wood's lack of upscale, traditional cachet makes it perfectly suited for today's comfortable gardens. Weathered birdhouses, bird feeders, painted cutouts of grazing sheep—even a hulking figure of a bear carved with a chain saw and bought from a roadside display—all lend a homi-ness and humor to planting beds that no marble statue could supply.

Cast resin, fiberglass, polypropylene, and related materials. These materials often lack the warmth of their natural counterparts, but where weight is an issue (as in the case of window boxes or large planters), they can be an effective choice.

Bronze lends itself to exuberant modern castings such as The Leap, *as well as to more staid, traditional designs.*

Wood figures bring a light-hearted touch to the garden.

A veil of rust covers this abstract steel face.

Cast-lead figures have graced gardens for centuries.

Wood has a down-home appeal that more expensive materials lack.

Lead cisterns have roots in England, where they were used during the seventeenth and eighteenth centuries to collect and store rainwater. Today, they still look most at home in English-style gardens. Many styles of cisterns were made and now are reproduced, including wall-hung cisterns fitted with taps.

French gardens once abounded with citrus trees, which were grown under glass during the winter in pots or wood-sided Versailles boxes.

Country of Origin

Geographic landmarks tell us about a garden's physical birthplace: the terrain that surrounds it and from which it arose. But there are cultural landmarks, too: ornaments that celebrate a gardener's ethnic heritage or national background, or that reflect an inborn affinity for gardens across the globe.

Artfully paired with appropriate plants and garden layout, these ornaments let us savor the gardens of the world without ever leaving home. A sundial set on a pillar of stone transports us to the rose-filled gardens of the British Isles; a snow-viewing lantern carved from granite carries us to the tranquil gardens of Japan; a tiled fountain conveys us to Portugal's sweet-scented courtyards. Such ornaments originally arose from the particular geography or iconography of their individual homeland, and through long association have become their hallmarks.

England. Although England has its formal landscapes, it is the country gardens of the British Isles that most inspire today's gardeners. Evoke their romantic atmosphere with sundials or armillary-sphere dials, Portland-stone sundial pillars, lead statuary, stone troughs, lead cisterns, millstones, basket-weave pots, floral finials, birdbaths, birdhouses, or chimney pots; mix with antique roses, clipped yews, flowering perennials. Think informal, abundant, romantic, and soft.

France. Put "France" and "garden" in the same sentence and most people think Versailles. Evoke the splendor of Louis's garden with bronze or marble statuary, baroque fountains, straight gravel paths, classical urns, and citrus trees in pots or boxes; mix with elaborate boxwood-edged parterres and geometric topiary. Think formal, expansive, flat, geometric, symmetrical, and rich.

*T*umbled columns and capitals, lying in a bed of forget-me-nots, bring to mind the days of ancient Rome and Greece: the golden age that Renaissance Italians vied to emulate. The stone monkeys allude to man's folly.

*F*luted columns serve as appropriate pedestals for classical-style busts, and also add an aura of antiquity to the garden on their own.

Alternately, evoke the simple, lavender-filled gardens of Provence with terra-cotta containers decorated with clusters of flowers or grapes or with the region's trademark glazed green pots (look for examples with fluted "pie crust" rims).

Italy. The Italian Renaissance spawned a garden style as enduring as its art and architecture. Evoke its theatricality with white marble statuary, Greek columns and capitals, fountains, urns, mosaic paving, high-relief Della Robbia-style ornament, round stone finials, or anything decorated with classical motifs; mix with cypress, cedars, boxwood-edged parterres, and topiary. Think formal but exuberant, with hints of irreverence and humor.

*G*lazed ceramic tile and a tiered fountain (above) inspire visions of sunny Portugal.

A central pool (right), still and reflective, encourages quiet contemplation.

*T*his geometric water feature carries the eye through the garden and refreshes the senses.

Islamic. Traditional gardens from Iran to India reflect the precepts of Islam; their water-filled courtyards form oases akin to Paradise in an arid and inhospitable world. Evoke their intricate symmetrical beauty with a central fountain or tank that brims with water and overflows into channels that divide the garden into quarters, symbolizing the rivers of Paradise. Limit decoration to geometric or intertwining patterns on paving or walls—the Koran prohibits figural ornament. Mix with an abundance of roses, narcissus, lilies, violets, and hollyhocks in square or rectangular parterres, and provide shade with poplar, plane, and fruit trees. Think enclosed, private, peaceful, and geometric, filled with color, scent, and birdsong.

Spain and Portugal. The Islamic culture of the Moors shaped the traditional courtyard gardens of the Iberian Peninsula, where water again plays a central role. Evoke their sunsplashed nature with tiled fountains, narrow water channels, brightly colored pots, painted urns, tiled murals, blue-and-white tile edgings, or geometric paving patterns; mix with bougainvillea, jasmine, myrtle, laurel, and orange trees. Think enclosed, private, sunny, and bright, cooled by the gurgle and splash of water.

Japan. Japanese gardens are known for their ability to capture the grandeur of nature in a limited space. Evoke their

"How often it is that a garden, beautiful though it be, will seem sad and dreary and lacking in one of its most gracious features, if it has no water."

—PIERRE HUSSON,
LA THEORIE ET LA PRATIQUE DU JARDINAGE, 1711

In Moorish gardens, the sound of splashing water echoed through lushly planted courtyards. This water channel reawakens their oasislike splendor.

OUT *of* PLACE

Although faraway gardens can provide welcome inspiration, wholesale copying of garden styles or the indiscriminate use of their hallmark ornaments does have pitfalls. The marble statuary of Italy, for instance, may look depressingly funereal under the cloudy skies of the Pacific Northwest, while England's lead cisterns cry out for roses, not cacti. Likewise, that Chinese garden may be lovely in theory but would look disturbingly out of place next to your California ranch home or Victorian-era farmhouse. (Your house, in essence, is the largest garden ornament you have, and it can't easily be ignored.)

When you divorce garden ornaments from their proper geographic or cultural context, you risk diminishing their power or making them clichés: the Japanese lantern next to the asphalt driveway, the miniature Dutch windmill amid the tulips, the statue of Neptune set in an arid rock garden rather than presiding over a spacious garden pool.

An ornament's function also must be considered in its placement. A sundial set in a leafy bower, for instance, is mere decoration, robbed of its time-telling potential. Although it's tempting to place a sundial or armillary-sphere dial where you can enjoy its form from the kitchen window or back porch, seek instead your sunniest garden spot. Before siting a dial, note the shadows cast by nearby trees, fences, and your house in both summer and winter seasons. Then pick the spot with the maximum solar power.

Large fountains, too, will benefit from sunny placement. Hidden away among the ferns and trees, their waterspouts and geysers lose their splendor. Smaller, naturalistic water features that gurgle and trickle suit shady woodland settings best.

In particular, take extra care when siting classical statues. Pan belongs in a shady vale, not in a sun-drenched parterre or suburban sideyard, and Diana deserves a woodland in which to hunt her stag.

"There is nothing adds so much to the Beauty and Grandeur of Gardens, as fine Statues; and nothing more disagreeable than when wrongly plac'd," wrote Batty Langley of Twickenham in 1728, a sentiment that still rings true after 270 years.

Finally, don't despair if you can't effectively reproduce your favorite garden style due to climate, water restrictions, budget, an ill-suited lot, or lack of access to authentic ornament. Instead, seek the essence of a style that appeals to you—the formality and order of a French garden, the tranquillity of a Japanese garden, the exuberance of an English cottage garden—and recreate it with ornament and plants better suited to your situation.

serenity with triads of rocks, stone water basins, stone lanterns, asymmetrical courses of stepping-stones, mosses and lichens, small ponds, raked gravel or sand, or dry waterfalls; mix with evergreens, camellias, azaleas, Japanese maples, wisteria, flowering plum, weeping cherry. Think small-scale, natural, tranquil, asymmetrical, contemplative, reverent, metaphoric, simple, and pure; include hidden views and special viewpoints.

China. Like the Japanese gardens they influenced, Chinese gardens traditionally have celebrated nature's strengths and many wonders. Evoke their drama with bizarre rock forms, ponds with carp, porcelain figures of lions and tigers, dragon or dragon-scale ornaments, sculptural plants in glazed containers, bonsai in low, rectangular trays set on stone tables or rough rock pedestals, gravel paths, rocks that look like animals or birds, zigzag pathways, raised stone beds, carved stone and pierced clay ornaments,

A stone lantern marks the way through a Japanese garden.

Bamboo and granite form a simple water feature.

Stepping-stones (above) wander in the garden, as in nature.

Raked sand (left) mimics water.

Planning for Ornament

The furnishing of a garden, like that of a house, happens over time. Of course, you can head out to the local garden center and stock up on statues, just as some people get their decorating over with by hauling in a load of brand-new chairs and sofas. But where's the pleasure in that? Better to wait for the perfect ornament to come along— at a tag sale or antique show, on a trip to Holland or Africa, or at a nursery in a neighboring town.

Then leave room in your garden for unexpected finds. Plan for a focal-point ornament in that bed of herbs, even though you haven't yet discovered the perfect sundial. Employ a rock as a space holder in a perennial bed, until you track down a birdbath that's suited to your taste. Go ahead and plant an evergreen backdrop for that marble bust you'd like to own someday. By the time you locate the version that matches your vision, the greenery will have grown into place.

stoneware fishbowls, or porcelain barrel-form garden seats; mix with bamboo, camellias, magnolias, wisterias, rhododendrons, peonies, chrysanthemums, pines, flowering trees, and China roses. Think natural; include hidden views and surprise scenes.

Although transplanted from its country of origin, any one of these ornaments can set a garden's tone—from homespun to exotic, regal to serene—simply by its unconscious associations. Consider how you want to feel when basking in your garden's glory—and choose your ornament accordingly.

Traversing the Gardener's Mind

Garden ornament reflects the outside world, both near and far away. But like the house you live in, the clothes you wear, or the words you speak, garden ornament can also set forth your personal style for all to see. Through well-chosen ornament you can signal your penchant for old-fashioned romance or elegant formality, or your passion for nature or art, as surely as if you'd

put it in print and posted a sign at the garden's front gate.

A birdbath, brimming with water fresh as morning, says you are a friend to warblers and jays and predicts a visit bouyed by birdsong and the whir of wings. Stone finials, carved in the shape of pineapples and set to flank a pair of steps, say you are a traditionalist and portend a visit marked by hospitality and social graces. A trio of granite boulders, set in a sea of moss and shaded by a gnarled pine, says you are a contemplative sort and predicts a time spent in quiet conversation and appreciation of nature's beauty. All are outward symbols of an inner state: shorthand for the gardener's soul.

What do you want your garden's ornament to say? Does it express your values and personal sense of style? If not, what might serve as your personal landmark in the garden, as potent in its way as Monet's wisteria-veiled bridge or the images of Apollo at Versailles? Search out the ornament that reflects who you are, and settle for nothing less.

The pineapple, here in the form of a weathered stone finial, symbolizes hospitality in the garden as well as in the house.

This simple birdbath (above) signals a passion for wildlife.

A Mexican maiden (left) imparts a sunny informality.

A dovecote (opposite) rides like an ark on waves of flowers.

EYE CATCHERS AND SPACE MAKERS

A BRONZE HERON SEARCHES FOR fish in a garden pond, while a carved rabbit plays hide-and-seek among the pines. Painted pots sprouting crowns of lavender march in pairs along a garden walk, while a flock of cast-stone pigeons search for seed among the bricks. All decorate the garden, providing a pleasing counterpoint to flowers, shrubs, trees, and ground covers. But they play other garden roles that belie their quiet nature.

Like highway signs and traffic signals, these ornaments tell us where to go and when to stop. They toy with our sense of the nearby and faraway, the minuscule and monumental, the spacious and confined. They dictate where we look.

A lifelike pig roots among the patio pavers; it draws the eye and brings a sense of humor to an otherwise formal garden space.

Curled in a carved-wood cave (opposite), this bear commands attention along a woodland path and emphasizes the wild beauty of the garden.

The music of a tiered cast-iron fountain calls to garden visitors and lures them into hidden garden spaces.

Few are the garden visitors who resent this gentle manipulation. Instead, we surrender without a thought, grateful for the guidance that ornament provides.

Creating Movement and Direction

Strolling through the garden, our feet seem to choose their own path. But in fact, it is the garden's ornaments that pull us along, from patch of lawn to perennial bed to dappled woodland glen.

A shaded stone figure at the end of a pathway seduces us as surely as a siren's song, and we willingly cover the intervening ground to meet up close. A trickle of water lures us around a well-trimmed hedge to glimpse a garden room and fountain tucked beyond. Up ahead, just visible through an arc of 'Old Blush' roses and past a shadowed court, a gabled birdhouse stands atop a six-foot pole: a Gothic cottage on a stick. We move toward it like kids toward candy, hungry for excess.

Figures placed at the outlying ends of pathways tug like magnets; their pull is hard to resist. The flagstone pathway leading to this painted figure slows the speed at which the eye travels toward it, and makes the journey seem as compelling as the destination.

GARDEN LESSONS

*N*ote the placement of urns and statuary in formal gardens.

*P*ay attention to the careful siting of contemporary works.

*D*on't hesitate to adapt ideas that strike a chord.

Don't just admire the plantings next time you're touring local gardens, strolling around a friend's backyard, or visiting Sissinghurst, the Villa d'Este, or Versailles. Instead, turn your attention to each garden's ornament.

Try to figure out what works, and why. What ornament draws your attention and pleases your eye? How is it positioned? Is it centrally located? Does it mark the junction of two pathways? Does it blend into a perennial bed or border of shrubbery? Does it lead your eye onward or terminate a view? How does its scale relate to the rest of the garden?

Note the predominant style of each ornament and the feeling it creates. Is it formal or informal, serious or humorous, modern or traditional, old or new? Does it establish a particular mood? Is it appropriate to the garden's prevailing style? Does its inclusion seem jarring, pretentious, or somehow out of place?

As you wander, take a look at the way each ornament is framed, and how its position alters its impact. Is that oil jar set on a plinth like the finest urn against a backdrop of close-clipped yew, or is it tipped on its side and overrun with nasturtiums? Do the plantings that surround it emphasize its character or detract from its appeal? Also take stock of the plinths and columns that support statues, busts, urns, and vases. What function do they serve?

Don't hesitate to jot down notes or take snapshots of the combinations you like. Back home, record ideas that stick with you and look for ways to work them into your own garden. The exact duplication of another garden's elements may not be possible (your friend's yard may be terraced and yours flat as a coffee table). But with time and keen observation, you'll be able to translate the successful marriage of plan, ornament, and planting in the gardens you visit into memorable garden scenes of your own.

Such ornaments provide destinations within the garden space, fruitful spots at which to linger and enjoy the garden's bounty. Other ornaments influence the choice of route from place to place, as well as the speed of the journey.

To move visitors toward a particular section of the garden, put pairs of ornaments to work. Basket finials, statues, or pots that flank a garden pathway become a sort of psychic gateway through which visitors feel compelled to pass. The same is true for a double row of columns or brick piers, or a pair of obelisks. To accelerate a visitor's passage, install smooth, straight walkways of brick or cut stone; to slow it down, provide a meandering course of stepping-stones or curved or zigzag gravel pathways. Variations of materials and plantings help put on the visual brakes, as do steps, gates, and alternating areas of light and shade.

More than any other device, multiple pairs of ornaments invite passage through the garden. For best effect, however, use only one type of object, such as oversized pots, simple obelisks, or statues of similar bearing.

This pair of somber busts, offset along a shady garden path, call visitors to explore the mysteries that lie unseen behind them.

A girl and her flock of lifesize geese (below) animate a distant corner of the garden and attract the gaze from far away.

Drawing the Eye

Our eyes are born wanderers, eager to roam but always grateful for a place to rest. On a city street, we scan the crowd until our eyes come to a stop on a child in a bright flowered dress or on a bunch of balloons held high above the masses. In the living room of a friend, our glance skips from place to place until it holds at a well-lit painting or a flower-filled vase. In the garden, the same is true. We unconsciously look for elements on which our eyes can linger—objects that emerge from the background by virtue of the following attributes.

Contrast. Although garden ornaments may be made from organic materials, they are neither plant nor flower nor tree, and therefore stand out amidst the greenery. Their solidity, permanence, and difference of form are apparent at a glance, whether the ornament in question is a Chinese stoneware fishbowl, an old wooden tub, or a bronze statue of a doe and fawn.

Arched in a typical feline pose, this sleek cat stands out among the flowers due to both its material and its stylized but true-to-life nature.

*T*he smallest trickle of water from a garden fountain catches the light and draws the eye, while its gurgling or splashing washes away all cares. This simple fountain evokes memories of mountain glens, where ferns sprout from between rocks to overhang a burbling spring. Even in the cool of fall, it refreshes.

*G*arden courtyards or other small spaces suit wall-mounted fountains best. This bronze lion's-head mask spouts a steady stream into inset basins below.

Movement. Motion is a magnet for the eye. The fountain's arc of water—a moving string of diamond droplets—instantly commands attention, as does the whirligig mounted on a fence post that waves its arms in the slightest breeze.

Size. Put an elephant in the garden and it's hard to ignore. So too are tub-size terra-cotta pots and hip-high oil jars, towering iron sunflowers, or a full-size replica of *The Thinker*. Don't be afraid to buy big. Likewise, pint-size ornaments, such as a tiny terra-cotta snail in a patio pot, grab more attention than their stature might suggest.

Position. Properly placed, ornament does more than draw the eye; it is an organizing element that can bring the garden itself into sharper focus. A cast-stone vase, enthroned on a plinth at the far end of the garden, can pull our glance across paved courtyard and grassy path, through gateways and up steps, forcing us to take in the garden as a whole. It is like the cross on a church steeple or the pediment over the doorway of a Georgian house: a fitting conclusion to all that has come before. Likewise, ornament that would be lost in this anchor position may serve to unify smaller garden sections, creating intimate garden pictures out of previously unrelated elements.

Because ornament catches the eye, the knowing gardener places it just where he or she wants viewers to look. Consider the vantage points from which your garden will be seen, then place your ornament to emphasize the garden's strengths.

First, pick a focal point, easily seen across the garden from your patio, dining-room window, or other favorite viewing spot.

A pair of bronze cranes, Japanese symbols of long life, point up the cascading nature of this garden as they wade through the foliage.

Similar cranes (above), standing at the edge of a pond, evoke an image of stillness and contemplation. Facing the water, they emphasize its placid presence.

An unadorned pedestal at the end of a garden path punctuates a stroll past globes of allium beneath a golden canopy.

In Good Company: Planting *to* Complement Ornament

Just as a well-placed statue brings focus to garden beds, well-chosen plants will enhance the desired effect of a cast-stone vase, a copper birdbath, or any other garden ornament. Plant and ornament are partners, playing off one another like moonlight on snow or sun on water.

Plants may repeat the horizontal or vertical form of a particular ornament, emphasizing its character from near or far away. They may contrast with an ornament's shape, and temper its dominant nature.

Clipped shrubberies echo the shape of a stone ball finial.

Plants may frame ornament, camouflage its flaws, bring it forward, cause it to recede, or soften its character. Likewise, certain plants—like stage sets—may provide the proper atmosphere for an ornament, whether it be beach grass springing through the bottom of a rotted-out rowboat, or giant leaves of gunnera shading the stalking figure of a giant cat.

TAKING STOCK

Before choosing companion plantings, analyze your ornament's visual character. Is it taller than wide, like a classical statue or obelisk? Or is it more horizontal in nature, like a birdbath or cast-stone pig? Does the ornament have a simple form, like a terra-cotta oil jar, or is it ornate in detail, like a replica of a classical frieze? What is the ornament's scale? Is it domineering or easily lost in a sea of foliage? Lastly, take stock of existing garden plantings that play roles similar to the ornament in question. Are there lots of vertical plants in your garden, such as hollyhocks or plumed ornamental grasses? Or is your garden's nature more horizontal? The answers to all these questions will help determine the new plant partners you pick.

PLANT PARTNERS

Vertical repetition or contrast. To emphasize an ornament's vertical nature, or to offset a horizontal ornament, choose plants with an up-and-down structure, such as iris, verbascum, crocosmia, daylily, multi-trunked trees, weeping trees, or bamboo.

Horizontal repetition or contrast. To echo an ornament's horizontal leanings or bring a soaring statue down to earth, choose plants with outward-reaching tendencies, such as bleeding heart, *Viburnum plicatum,* dogwood, cotoneaster, Japanese maple, or creeping mahonia. Mounding plants also emphasize horizontal or rounded ornament forms.

Background. Some ornaments need to be set off from the garden at large, like pictures in a frame. Marble statuary, in particular, needs a simple backdrop: a clipped alcove of yew, a monochrome frame of evergreen rhododendron, or a wall cloaked with English ivy or Virginia creeper. Less formal ornaments aren't as choosy about their setting and will look equally at home with a riot of perennials or a stately backdrop of privet or boxwood. As a general rule, the simpler the form of the ornament, the busier the

This somber face takes on an air of mystery behind oversized foliate fans.

Vines bind a stone head as if in the deepest jungle.

Sun-loving thyme makes itself at home around a garden sundial.

plantings around it can be.

Camouflage. Ornament takes on an air of mystery when partially obscured from sight by an outstretched branch or a cloak of vines. In addition, judicious screening can camouflage a multitude of sins: the poor proportions of a statue, the crack in a cast-stone urn, the rough concrete column that supports a silvered sphere.

Grounding. Effective ornament looks at home in the garden, as wedded to the soil as the shrubs and the trees. Ground-hugging or spreading plants such as euonymus, nepeta, lamb's ears, snow-in-summer, bergenia, St. John's wort, or artemisia help tie an ornament to the earth, obscuring the line between the ornament's base and the soil or foundation beneath.

White wisteria stands out next to the gray of a lead urn.

A sensuous but simple jar provides the perfect foil for a multitextured profusion of blossoms and foliage.

Horizontal branches contrast with an obelisk's upright form.

Twining ivy crowns a child's head and binds her to the earth.

Position. The color and texture of plants around a garden ornament affect how we perceive the ornament's position in space. Cool-toned plants, such as those with blue flowers or shrubs and trees with blue-gray foliage, make an ornament seem to recede, as do plants with fine-textured foliage or small leaves, such as abelia, deutzia, choisya, some ceanothus, and most ever-greens. Alternately, flowers or leaves with warm color tones or with bold leaves (such as oak-leaf hydrangea, some rhododendrons, and hostas) bring an ornament forward in space and make it the center of attention.

Character. When choosing companion plants, consider the ornament's dominant mood or dramatic character. A weathered rocker without its seat will look like a candidate for the landfill if positioned next to a formal hedge. But tucked in the shade and overrun with euonymus, it adds a nostalgic grace note to the garden. In the same manner, a pyramid of stainless steel will resemble industrial waste dropped in a bed of English roses. But set on a gravelly plain and surrounded by spiky phormium or upright verbascum, its spare character seems right at home.

Leaves and blossoms that partially obscure an ornament add to its allure and blend it gracefully into the garden.

Puffs of allium and frills of kale accent a shapely earthenware jar.

Pink yarrow forms a sweet bed for a garden cherub.

"*Statues are commend-
able in the midst of Fountains, and Green Squares,
in Groves, and at the ends
of obscure walks.*

*Other ancient Orna-
ments of a Garden are
Flower-pots, which
painted white and placed
on Pedestals, either on
the ground in a streight
line on the edges of your
Walks, or on your Walls,
. . . are exceeding
pleasant.*"

—JOHN WORLIDGE,
SYSTEMA HORTICULTURAE,
1677

*Placed at the far end of the
garden, this graceful figure pulls
the eye across the intervening
space. Her bowed head gives her
a quiet air, while she raises her
shift as if to gather flowers.*

Place the most dominant ornament there. Choose such a focal-point ornament with care; it must be strong enough, and large enough, to justify its position as the center of attention.

If you want to draw the eye across the garden and include the view beyond, place the focal-point ornament at the far end of the garden. If you want to keep attention focused within the garden space and away from its edges, choose a central spot. If your focal-point ornament seems too small, raise it to eye level on a plinth or pillar. If it seems too big, blend it into the garden by wrapping it with climbing vines, shading it, or allowing other plants or tree branches to slightly obstruct the line of sight between you and it.

Once the focal-point ornament is in position, employ lesser ornaments to draw attention to that graceful old apple tree or bed

This elaborate stone urn draws attention to a row of neatly pleached hornbeams. Like classical statuary, such heavily modeled pieces look best against a simple backdrop.

of true geraniums. Keep in mind what you *don't* want garden visitors to notice—the overflow outlet for the sewer line or the nursery bed where you keep your ailing plants—and direct their gaze to other sections of the garden.

A Sense of Space

It's a refrain adapted from a familiar tale. This garden is TOO big. This garden is TOO small. This garden is JUST right. Like Goldilocks, we know automatically whether our garden satisfies our individual need for space—no tape measure is required.

Although we rarely can do anything to change the physical dimensions of our allotted plot (short of annexing the neighbor's yard), we can alter the *perceived* sense of space through carefully placed ornament.

Consider a single square garden at the rear of a house. To make it seem longer, plan a straight walkway from back door to back hedge, and place a focal-point ornament at its end. Emphasize the walk with low hedges or flower borders, punctuated at

Set at the edge of a scalloped basin, this statue of a kneeling child draws attention to the water as viewers follow the child's downward gaze.

ON STAGE

Set a statue, urn, or herb-filled pot on the ground in the garden and it somehow lacks impact. But raise it up on a plinth or pedestal and it becomes a focal point, a garden star on stage.

Traditionally, gardeners have chosen plinths and pedestals made from marble, limestone, or cast stone, but all these can be costly. Instead of breaking your ornament budget on mere underpinnings, it's possible to make your own supports.

Construct a simple pedestal by assembling an open-ended box from ½-inch or ¾-inch plywood, reinforced at the inside corners with lengths of 2 × 2-inch lumber. If desired, tack plain or decorative molding into place at the outside corners to camouflage the seams. Seal or paint the box to ward off moisture, then set it on a flat paver and top with another paver or a square of painted wood. Set the ornament on top.

You can also make low plinths by stacking fieldstones, ceramic pavers, bricks, or concrete blocks on top of one another, or by stacking groups of terra-cotta pots. If your garden has a woodsy bent, put sawed-off tree stumps to work. Or use squat pieces of clay sewer pipe as pedestals, stablized with flat ceramic pavers at the tops and bottoms.

Most of these supports will blend gracefully into the garden if you mask them with appropriate mounding or vining plants.

Alternately, if your woodworking or masonry skills are up to speed, you can construct wood-paneled pedestals or piers of mortared brick or stone that will do justice to even the most formal garden setting.

Note: Heavy ornaments should not be set on lightweight supports, particularly if they have antique value. Instead, provide a level concrete footing and a stone, brick, or cast-stone plinth or pedestal. Both the support structure and the ornament should be cemented in place.

A simple pillar raises an urn to new heights.

Gargoyles need a lofty perch so they can be seen from below.

Without its pillar, this urn would be swallowed by foliage.

regular intervals with cast-stone urns, terra-cotta jars, or other pairs of ornaments. Crisscross the main walk with perpendicular pathways and have it pass beneath an arbor or pergola, or through a gap in a hedge. Use more than one paving material: brick interrupted with bands of cobblestones, or gravel with a stone border. The more the eye has to notice as it sweeps down the walk, the more distant the end of the garden will seem.

To further stretch the garden's length, exaggerate the sense of perspective. Taper the walkway so it's narrower at the far end than it is near the house (experiment with what looks natural, using stakes and twine). Lessen the space between one pair of ornaments and the next as they get closer to the rear of the garden. Likewise, place larger ornaments in the foreground of the garden and smaller ones toward the back. Just remember: tricks such as these are most effective when your garden is more likely to be looked at than walked through. Such forced perspective can look disconcertingly odd from the wrong end.

You can make that same square garden seem larger overall by carving it into smaller pieces. Divide the garden into separate square planting beds, defined by a simple geometric ornament at each corner. Plant hedges and put up trellises to form separate garden rooms, then furnish each with its own focal-point ornament. Or lay out curving pathways that carry you from one unseen section of the garden to the next, discovering new ornament along the way. When garden wanderers can't glimpse the whole scheme at once, they can imagine it going on forever.

If cozy intimacy rather than expansion is your goal, keep the attention focused on the garden's center. Install a flagstone patio with central fountain, wellhead, sundial, or armillary-sphere dial, or leave the space open for a table and comfortable chairs. Ring

In this garden, the viewer's gaze must travel past plants and through a gatelike opening before reaching its final destination: a stone sphere. Such visual interruptions expand a garden's sense of space.

Subtle manipulations of perspective, such as a slightly tapered walkway or arches of diminishing size, make a modest garden seem palatial.

A trompe l'oeil painting on a potting shed door fools the eye and hints at the pots and garden tools—and owls— that wait within.

Though this wall (above) is flat, cleverly angled latticework conjures up an alcove behind a stately urn.

An ornate jar brings focus to this tiny garden, a gem lined by roses and germander and carpeted with chamomile.

the patio with a collection of colorful containers, from glazed pots to painted planter boxes. Reverse the perspective trick, and place larger ornament at the far end of the garden and smaller ornament in the foreground. Further enhance the garden's inward-looking feel by mounting decorative terra-cotta plaques or wall-hung fountains on the garden's walls or fences, or by facing statuary looking in toward the garden's heart.

Similar strategies can be adopted no matter what your garden's size or shape. Place a stone lantern along a sinuous pathway through a narrow side yard, and notice the effect on your passage. Build a dovecote at the far corner of a broad backyard, and observe how it changes your sense of space. Visit public gardens, and note how the ornaments catch your eye, alter your experience, and guide you on your journey.

Like a painter's brushes or a sculptor's chisels, such ornaments—though beautiful in form—are among a gardener's most serviceable tools. Don't hesitate to put them to work.

HEAVENLY SPHERES

Once held in the same regard as plastic flamingos and garden pinwheels, gazing globes now captivate a new generation of gardeners. These silvered spheres, available in a rainbow of tints, distill the world around them into a single magic image, odd as a face in a funhouse mirror and entrancing as the future in a soothsayer's crystal ball.

Warm as the sun, this globe reflects the hues of fall.

Victorian gardeners adored their shimmer and often set a gazing globe upon a pedestal at the heart of the garden, where it captured bright images of cannas, salvias, heliotrope, and looming garden statuary, along with a brilliant wash of sky. Gardeners today are often more inventive. One may ring her garden with a necklace of gazing globes, each lifted above the ground by a slender metal support. Another may nestle a golden globe like an Easter egg among ornamental grasses to magnify their autumn hues, or tuck a globe, like a quicksilver pool, at the base of a thicket of ferns. Other gardeners may suspend their gazing globes from the branches of trees, like giant Christmas ornaments, echoing their alleged early indoor use as hanging "witches balls" or "wish balls." (One was thought to ward off evil; the other was a gift symbolizing best wishes for a long and prosperous life.)

Gazing globes are available today at many garden shops and through mail-order catalogs, and generally come in 10-inch, 12-inch, and 14-inch sizes. Alternatives, which lack the gazing globes' gleam yet retain the magic of the spheres, include glass fishing floats (launched in a birdbath or fountain), marbles (scattered in a garden bed), stone ball finials (cemented on the brick piers of a garden wall), or even bowling balls (rolled among the hostas or the sedums).

Note: Birdbath pedestals make excellent supports for gazing globes and other spheres.

This globe shimmers like a bit of sky fallen to the earth.

A silvered globe captures the entire garden in its sphere.

WORKING ORNAMENT

ALL ORNAMENT HAS A JOB TO DO, from delighting the eye to giving shape or focus to the garden. But some ornaments participate more actively than others in garden life. They cater to wildlife or coddle our transplants. They scare off marauding crows or lift up our lima beans. They sprinkle our pansies or shower our tomatoes. They come to the garden to fulfill a need, and remain as honored guests.

These garden laborers have their own compelling beauty, impossible to divorce from their daily duties. A glass cloche, for instance, sits in the garden like a tiny temple, a jewel in the morning sun. But one can't dwell on its bell-like form without thinking of the tender seedlings it protects from untimely frosts, or the cuttings it coaxes to take root later in the season. Likewise, a bird feeder built from scraps of cedar shingle is inseparable from the chickadees it supplies with seed throughout the year; its form alone has come to represent their feathered charm.

*S*tand-ins for the gardener, scarecrows bring touches of humanity and ingenuity to the garden. This aproned matron fusses over the lettuce and onions as if they were her children.

*A*n old pump (opposite) stands firm amidst the foxgloves and the calla lilies, recalling days before hoses and water wands. Such working relics provide a connection to gardeners of the not-so-distant past.

*E*ngulfed by the glories of
spring, this scalloped cement
birdbath calls attention to
a river of forget-me-nots.
Fledglings hatched from nests
in nearby trees will find this a
convivial spot to bathe, particularly since it's out in the open.

*V*enerable copper boilers, zinc
pots, or galvanized troughs
brimming with rainwater are
perfect for dip-filling a watering
can when plants need a drink.

That there is beauty in usefulness is hardly a new concept; the
idea was acknowledged by the ancient Greeks and has been pro-
moted by countless writers since. Like the importance of healthy
soil or the value of a good spade, it's an idea that has proved its
mettle in gardens throughout time.

Welcome Wildlife

When naturalist Mark Catesby roamed the Carolinas during the
early 1700s, he noted how the Choctaw and Chickasaw Indians
hung birdhouses made from gourds around their gardens to
attract purple martins: voracious eaters of mosquitoes and garden
pests. Most birds—from larks and blue jays to finches and
robins—weren't so well treated. So abundant were these and
other species that native tribes and European settlers were far
more apt to *eat* them than to provide them with shelter or suste-
nance. "Four and twenty blackbirds, baked in a pie" wasn't just a
rhyme—it was a recipe.

By the early 1900s, however, with flocks decimated by market hunters and nesting grounds fast disappearing, the birds' lilting songs, flitting charm, and huge appetite for insects began to be missed. "Save our birds" became the rallying cry of fledgling bird clubs across the country.

Today, we benefit from the legacy of that early conservation movement. Birdbaths, bird feeders, and birdhouses of all descriptions are widely available, and once in place, foster a vitality in the garden that plants alone cannot supply. What gardener doesn't thrill to see an acorn woodpecker balanced on the edge of the birdbath, a wren emerging from its tiny house, or a gold finch feasting on sunflower seeds at the feeder? The birds' lively beauty isn't their only gift; the more we make them feel at home, the more likely we'll have flocks of white-crowned sparrows devouring seeds of pesky spurge in our garden beds, or warblers snatching leaf-chomping larvae from our roses.

Water surges over a smooth disc of stone, inviting warblers and sparrows to splash and drink their fill.

Tucked among the azaleas and bergenias, a granite basin (above) serves up water to frogs, salamanders, and birds, as well as thirsty pets.

Hewn from granite, this rustic birdbath (left) seems part of the natural world it serves.

HOUSE HUNTING

Decorative birdhouses abound, from quaint cottages with painted curtains at the windows to gleaming constructions of copper and weathered wood. But if you want to ensure tenants—from wrens to woodpeckers—keep the following features in mind.

Elbow room. Different birds prefer different sizes of nest boxes and entry holes. Titmice, nuthatches, and downy woodpeckers like 4-inch-deep and -wide boxes that are 8- to 10-inches high. Entry holes should be 1¼ inches in diameter. House wrens like a shorter, 6- to 8-inch-high box. Chickadees prefer a smaller entrance of 1⅛ inches; nuthatches an entrance of 1⅜ inches. Place entrance holes 6 to 8 inches up from the base, and secure boxes 5 to 15 feet from the ground (no higher than 10 feet for wrens). Robins prefer an open nesting shelf: an 8-inch-wide, 7-inch-deep shelf, with three 8-inch-high sides, placed 6 to 15 feet high.

Welcome mat. A rough patch below the entry hole—inside and out—helps birds come and go. A perch simply gives birds such as starlings and house sparrows a place to sit while they heckle more desirable occupants.

Shelter from storms. A steeply pitched roof with ample overhang will keep rain at bay, while holes drilled in the nest-box floor will allow any rain that blows inside to drain away.

Breathing lessons. If the birdhouse you buy doesn't have air vents (holes or gaps where the roof and walls meet), drill some holes beneath the roof overhang.

Room with a view. The best nest boxes have a hinged or removable top or side that allows you to peek inside, and that gives easy access for cleaning chores once the fledglings have left the nest. (Wire this tightly closed when birds are nesting to protect them from predators.)

A sturdy roof protects tenants of this simple house.

Old paint and a faded flag add cachet to a steepled birdhouse.

Even a basic box can lure homeless birds to nest.

A miniature church ministers to an avian sort of flock.

This avian pavilion provides temporary shelter.

Elderflowers shelter this bird-house from the summer sun.

A pint-size dovecote draws attention from a distance.

WE HAVE THIS ONE!

Saltbox styling suits birds as well as it does New Englanders.

An elegant apartment house beckons gregarious birds.

A fence smothered in roses takes on a gracious dimension with the addition of a simple white birdhouse.

Birds provide garden ornament without parallel, particularly at the birdbath. Shallow baths such as this one allow even hulking ravens to quench their thirst, while small species such as eastern bluebirds can drink, splash, and wade to their heart's content—all without danger of drowning.

The thrill of watching parents tend to their nestlings (above) more than compensates for the minimal cleaning and upkeep a nest box requires.

This gnarled chair (right), with its nest and birdhouse finials, seems rooted in place.

A plain ceramic birdbath that reflects the blue of sky or a tiny cedar nest box nailed to the backyard fence may be all the ornament some gardens need (the birds themselves will supply the rest). More formal gardens may benefit from fancier baths made from cast stone, bronze, or glazed ceramic, or from multi-room martin houses or elaborate feeders built from barn board and weathered scraps of copper. Some gardeners also put out the welcome mat for other insectivores, such as bats and toads, or for pollinators such as orchard mason bees and butterflies. Houses for all are available, along with traditional straw bee skeps and shelves for luring nesting phoebes or robins.

Even when the flock has flown, the fledglings have left the nest, and the bees have holed up for the winter, these baths, feeders, and houses lend a sense of unstinting hospitality to any garden.

BECKONING *the* BEES

It's a simple domed basket, turned upside down and set on a stool in the middle of the garden. Yet the traditional straw bee skep is more than a pleasing ornament. Its wheat-straw coils recall a timeless relationship between man and bee that has sweetened our puddings, cured our coughs, illuminated our homes and churches, salved our wounds, and preserved our perishables. All that, and pollinated our fruits and flowers, too.

The straw bee skep symbolizes industry and plenty.

A shingled roof protects this apiary from heat and rain.

A traditional herb garden often had a skep at its heart.

Today, few garden bee skeps vibrate with the drone of an active swarm, busy building combs and storing amber honey. (The use of traditional skeps is prohibited in many states because the hives can't readily be inspected.) But prior to the nineteenth century, gardens throughout Europe and in much of America boasted such active bee baskets, often set on benches and protected from rain by wood or thatched roofs. Straw skeps that were "large and deep and even-proportioned like a Sugarloaf" were particularly favored (according to William Lawson in 1617) because they were easy to move about and kept their residents dry and warm.

Replicas of early straw skeps are most evocative of times past when set in the herb garden (honey made from thyme, lavender, and rosemary blossoms has been cherished since ancient times), or beneath the boughs of a blossoming fruit tree. Follow tradition and set your skep on a wooden stool to stymie the mice, or build a simple roofed bench and set up your own apiary with a trio of skeps. With luck, these symbols of productivity and sweetness will make honeybees (whose populations are dwindling at an alarming rate) feel at home in your garden, even if they don't move in.

Hardworking ornaments in this garden include bamboo plant stakes, terra-cotta row markers, a wheeled wooden cart, and a galvanized trash can that harbors potatoes.

A wooden wheelbarrow (below), parked beneath the wisteria, is both functional and beautiful.

Replicas of antique edging tiles define the edge of a gravel pathway. Reproductions of other edging designs also are available.

Lightening the Load

Other ornament caters to the gardener and the plants—rather than to wildlife—bringing beauty's leavening effect to our every-day chores. A ceramic hose pot keeps the hose neatly coiled and the vinyl under wraps; its simple form is as graceful as an ancient urn. A wrought-iron bootscraper puts mud in its place when the gardening day is done, while plant markers—whether ribbons of copper or terra-cotta fleur-de-lis—put us on a first-name basis with the occupants of our beds and borders.

Additional opportunities for useful ornament abound. There are flowerbed edgings, cast from terra-cotta or tinted concrete, which replicate popular nineteenth century rope designs, along with low willow fences that recall Victorian "basket" edgings (both keep garden paths and beds well defined). There are bronze sprinklers shaped like frogs, boot brushes shaped like bristly hedgehogs or seals, and cast-brass faucets with handles shaped like sunflowers or quail. There are cast-aluminum hose hangers in fancy palmette designs, as well as cast-iron or concrete bed fenders and hose guides, with decorative finials that prevent vulnerable plants from becoming casualties in the tug-of-war of watering.

But it is in the vegetable or kitchen garden that function and beauty are most naturally entwined.

During the Victorian era, kitchen gardens on large estates were sequestered behind massive brick walls, their carrots and cabbages deemed too mundane for public view. But many a gentleman or gentlewoman bucked convention and retreated to the kitchen garden's neatly graveled walks, seeking a refreshing simplicity of form and design not found in formal gardens of the times.

A regiment of glass cloches marches through the garden. Glass bells like these have seen service in the garden for centuries, protecting seedlings from frost and helping cuttings to take root. Antique cloches are a prized find, but even reproductions bring a taste of old traditions to the vegetable plot.

Terra-cotta forcers also can protect young plants from frost (or sun), but their historic role in the garden was twofold. First, they were used to force crowns of sea kale and rhubarb into winter growth; and second, they blanched these taste treats as sprouts emerged.

Relatives of the glass cloche or bell glass, hand glasses were, in essence, miniature greenhouses that gardeners could shift around as their protection was required.

A sturdy trellis for sweet peas serves as a rustic obelisk and provides a vertical accent for a low-lying vegetable garden.

Now, as then, the pure functionality of the kitchen or vegetable garden pleases the eye; the neatly spaced rows and beds express a logic hard to grasp in other garden schemes. There are no fancy parterres, only the trim cold frames with their panes of glass, the feathery asparagus beds, the berry vines and rambling squash—each producing its harvest in successive season.

Yet, ornament abounds. A trio of fat terra-cotta forcers, once used for bringing rhubarb and sea kale shoots to winter life, stand like overprotective nannies in the summer garden, ready at a moment's notice to shelter transplants from the wilting sun. A cherry clack, propeller awhirl, makes a racket even blackbirds can't endure, deterring them from devouring ripening fruit. And a fat French watering can, its oval bottom rusted away, sits on a garden bench: mute testimony to a nursery's worth of seedlings watered and grown on. Even a well-worn spade, briefly left standing in the garden, becomes a fitting ornament and evokes the labors of gardeners past.

Look around. There's probably working ornament in your garden already, from spiraling metal tomato stakes and overflowing rain barrels to a picturesque iron handpump or pile of old pots.

If not, deploy a scarecrow amid your 'Starshine' sweet corn, with tufts of hay escaping from its faded 501s. Build bamboo tepees for your green beans, establishing a cool retreat for picking beneath the pyramid of vines. Or anchor a weathered ladder at the garden's center and send nasturtiums climbing skyward.

Artistic masterworks they're not: just honest laborers among the garden's many glories. But they satisfy the senses all the same.

A sleek, speckled bird forms the handle on a garden spigot.

This weighty garden roller once leveled paths and lawns.

ELEVATING *the* POT

When it comes to garden ornament, pots and other containers work harder than almost any other type. Not only are containers decorative in their own right, dressing up stark patios, steps, and garden walls, but they also provide a movable home for any number of garden plants, from succulent strawberries to exotic *Cordyline australis*.

Basket-weave pots and a shapely jar represent the tip of the iceberg when it comes to garden containers.

Though modest in scale, pots have a history as old as the pyramids. Tomb paintings in Egypt depict plants growing in ornamental clay pots; clay containers coddled plants in ancient China and Japan; and decorated terra-cotta pots were popular outdoor ornaments in ancient Greece and Rome. On wealthy European estates during the seventeenth and eighteenth centuries, costly orange and lemon trees were even grown outdoors in oversized pots or wood boxes during summer's warmth, then wheeled inside the protection of a heated, glass-fronted *orangerie* at the first sign of frost. But it wasn't until the nineteenth century, as exotic plants imported from temperate lands became must-have items for every Victorian garden, that container gardening—as we know it today—became a standard part of the home gardener's repertoire.

Today, containers of one sort or another remain the garden's most popular ornament, from halved whiskey barrels lush with crops of tender lettuce or fragrant sweet peas to reproduction cast-stone urns sporting prickly crowns of agave. Along with traditional containers, gardeners also plant up claw-foot bathtubs, old wash tubs, tin cans, cast-iron cauldrons, even old boots—in short, anything that will contain a pocketful of fertile soil and sustain a healthy fringe of roots.

CHOOSING A CONTAINER

Keep the following attributes in mind when choosing containers for the garden.

Size. The bigger the better is the general rule. Large pots and containers make a strong visual impression in the garden, and they don't dry out as fast as small pots, which may need watering more than once a day. To lessen the weight of a tall container, as well as the expense of filling it with potting soil, fill it partway with crocks—broken pieces of old pots—or other rubble.

Material. Terra-cotta is the top vote getter; it blends easily into almost any garden style, develops a pleasing patina of moss or a frosty veil of efflorescence with time, and comes in a wide range of styles. Look for pots that have a nice ring—rather than a thud—when tapped, and that don't leave terra-cotta dust on your fingers. Glazed stoneware tubs and pots bring added color to the garden and aren't as fragile as their terra-cotta cousins, but they won't develop a patina with age. In general, steer clear of plastic or

A chimney pot's multiple pockets lend a foothold to sempervivums.

A simple wooden barrow spills geraniums and petunias.

A cast-iron urn erupts with 'Comptesse de Bouchard' clematis.

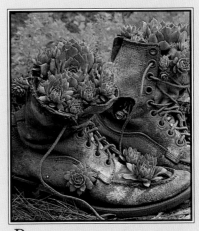

Rosettes of sempervivum sprout from a worn pair of boots.

Wire plant holders thrilled Victorian gardeners.

Patterned terra-cotta suits a Southwestern arrangement.

Ram's heads form handles on a massive, upright vase, which wears a cap of pink pelargoniums.

unplanted; the same goes for cast-iron urns and vases from the Victorian era (who wants to cover up their classical beauty with overgrown plants?). Cast-stone replicas, however, can be planted in good conscience. Because of their weight, these work well as permanent garden features. It's also possible to find replicas of antique pots and urns made from cast resin or fiberglass. Both are lightweight and often have an appealing antiqued finish, but they aren't hospitable to the softening effects of mosses or lichens.

Style. Covet a simple country garden? Choose plain-Jane terra-cotta pots, wooden tubs or half-barrels, low stoneware tubs, or sturdy baskets lined first with moss and then with plastic. Want the warmth of the Mediterranean? Choose colorful earthenware pots glazed in cobalt blue, green, or ocher, pots with fluted pie-crust rims, or simple terra-cotta jars and pots. Is your style more formal? Look to wooden Versailles-type boxes (painted white or green), classical urns of cast stone, or terra-cotta pots decorated with floral swags or basket-weave patterns. Seek the serenity of the East? Opt for glazed stoneware bowls and dishes, decorated or plain.

polypropylene pots colored to resemble terra-cotta; although inexpensive and lightweight (clear advantages over traditional clay pots), they will always look somewhat lifeless in the garden.

Wood wins for large planters and traditional Versailles-type boxes, which are great for showcasing patio trees, rose or bay standards, or the traditional orange or lemon tree. Teak, redwood, western red cedar, and lenga (a Chilean hardwood that's easier on the pocketbook than teak) last longest. To extend the life of wooden planters, use plastic or galvanized metal liners and paint the wood or treat it with preservative. Be sure to allow for drainage.

Antique stone or lead urns (if you're lucky enough to own one) often are best left

A bowl-shaped urn overflows with fuzzy helichrysum.

Shadows emphasize the heavy modeling on this urn.

Striking hues of foliage and blossom, from begonias and dahlias to chocolate cosmos, complement the colors of moss and terra-cotta.

Shape. Rimless terra-cotta pots in the traditional tapered form recall English country gardens of the last century. Sensuously rounded oil jars and small-necked amphorae have an ancient lineage, but these utilitarian vessels once used for storing olives, wine, and oil are latecomers to the garden and aren't really designed for planting. If you do plant in any sort of nar-row-necked vessel, make sure to use annuals without extensive root systems. Perennials with tenacious roots can be difficult to extract from the confines of the container when it's time to replant. Shallow, footed urns originated in classical times; they take on a particularly romantic air when planted with trailing specimens such as variegated ivy, lobelia, vinca, or campanula.

Set off taller urns or vases with a puffy crown of plants or with vertical growers such as ornamental grasses.

PLANTING CONTAINERS
Container gardens need a little more of everything than the average earthbound garden: more drainage, more frequent watering and feeding—even more plants. Keep these pointers in mind as you plant those pots.

Low-growing herbs soften an antique lead cistern.

A graceful niche frames a special terra-cotta vase.

Drainage. Make sure the container has ample drainage. If possible, raise the container above the ground or patio surface with terra-cotta-pot feet, flat rocks, bricks, boards, or the like. Provide drainage holes in the container's base if there are none, or fill the container one-third full with broken crockery, loose stones, or other coarse rubble and add a layer of unmilled sphagnum peat moss before filling with soil mix. Keep drainage holes from clogging with dirt by placing potsherds, concave side down, over them. Don't allow pots to sit in saucers of water; the roots of the plant will drown.

Soil mix. Fill containers with a mix of one part screened compost, one part milled Canadian sphagnum peat moss, and one part sharp builder's sand or perlite (popped volcanic ash). Or use a purchased potting soil mix. If desired, add organic fertilizers such as kelp meal, bonemeal, or blood meal to increase long-term fertility. Moisten the mix well and let sit overnight before adding plants. Be sure to soak terra-cotta pots in water before planting in them; likewise, set potted nursery plants in a tub of water to thoroughly moisten soil before transplanting them to their new decorative container.

Plants. There are as many ways to plant pots as there are gardeners. Some gardeners limit plantings to one type of plant per container, then create a textured effect by grouping pots together. Others create jewellike miniature gardens in a single large pot. Where one gardener may prefer a pot bright with annuals, another may mix bulbs, perennials, annuals, and vines, layering the bulbs in the pot as the other plants are added. Whatever your leaning, don't skimp on plant material; pots need a profusion of plants to fulfill their decorative potential. Even if a single plant forms the container's focus, such as a lollipop-like standard of bay or rose, or a dwarf lemon tree, don't miss the chance to underplant with thyme, catmint, Johnny jump-ups, or pansies.

Care and feeding. Because many plants share a limited amount of soil in a pot, they gobble up available nutrients faster than other garden occupants. Feed plants in containers with a liquid fertilizer such as fish emulsion, diluted to the directed strength, every two weeks. Likewise, soil in pots and containers will dry out faster than soil in garden beds (terra-cotta pots in particular are prone to quick drying). Small pots may need to be watered as frequently as twice a day in hot weather; larger containers should be checked every few days. If small pots dry out completely, immerse them in a tub of water until the soil is thoroughly soaked, then allow excess water to drain. If larger containers are completely parched, you may need to

An ovoid jar sprouts a tangle of sweet peas and pansies.

Artful pots support clambering roses and clematis.

This cast-stone pot and its rose standard merge into the surrounding garden, where fat heads of hydrangeas reign.

poke holes in the soil mix to get the water to penetrate rather than simply run down the inside walls of the container and out the bottom.

Positioning. Fill containers near the house or on the patio with fragrant plants such as heliotrope or old-fashioned roses, or with the thyme, parsley, oregano, and tarragon you need regularly in the kitchen. For windy spots, consider filling heavy clay pots with clipped balls of rosemary, box, or scented geraniums, or with single specimens of lavender or germander. Locate top-heavy container plantings such as standards or small trees in protected positions in the garden to avoid wind damage.

Timing. For best results when using a variety of plants, replant containers twice a year, changing soil completely. Even perennials in pots will appreciate a change of soil once a year. If the root ball of the plant fills the pot, and you don't want to move the plant to a larger container, carefully cut away an inch or two of roots around the sides and bottom of the root ball. Put new soil in the bottom of the pot, lower the plant into place, then add new soil around the sides and firm into place.

OUT OF SEASON

URING SUMMER'S SUN-DRENCHED days, when the garden is at its peak, the blooms of clematis, coneflower, rose, and hollyhock are the garden's shining stars. Ornament, for the most part, plays only a supporting role. But during the off-season, when fall strips the garden of its finery and spring has yet to fully blossom, it is ornament that commands the stage. Its steadfast strength lends beauty to garden walks, courtyards, and flower borders even when branches are bare and a wayward cardinal provides the only splash of color.

Think of a single waist-high stone, set like a gem in the middle of the garden. At summer's peak, it is lost in a sea of foliage. But come fall its latent power is revealed. Its slow emergence from hiding emphasizes the loss of each surrounding leaf, until the stone rises naked as a breaching whale from a sea of gold. When

Frost highlights the stark geometry of a garden's boxwood hedges and cools a dial's sunny disposition.

The chill breath of a winter's morning transforms the barren garden (opposite) into a thing of beauty: all silver filigree, mist, and icy lace.

A rain-wet rock juts from the earth behind a tangle of blackened branches. Such natural ornament highlights the shifts in the seasons.

Fog brings a gentle hush to the garden (above). And when all around is muted and still, even inanimate statues seems infused with potential life.

Easy to overlook in summer or fall, this statue's chilly imagery gains potency when temperatures plummet.

rain streams down its face it turns to polished ebony; as fierce winds blow, it stands fast while the rest of the garden falters. When snow crowns its head it seems as timeless as an ancient standing stone—a marker of unknowable meaning—while in spring, it shelters newborn hyacinths and daffodils, a stern but loving guardian of nature's fledgling glories.

It's not just that the stone or any other ornament is there, giving the garden structure and interest while the plants come and go (although that is part of its appeal). Equally important is that the stone, by virtue of its permanence, opens our eyes to each

A dusting of snow turns every stem and seedpod into a garden ornament while it temporarily outlines an armillary-sphere sundial in softest white.

Clay forcers, arrayed in the kitchen garden, say that winter has arrived. Like cocoons, they shelter developing plants from the effects of snow and frost.

subtle increment of change throughout the seasons. We are more apt to notice the falling leaves, the rain, the snow, the tender growth because the stone is there; it is the immutable gauge by which the rhythmic life of the garden is measured.

Choosing Seasonal Ornament

Any permanent garden ornament will act as a foil to nature's fluctuations, heightening our ability to appreciate the perpetual cycle of growth and decline and savor the season's beauty. But some ornaments are more effective at this role than others, particularly at certain times of year.

For centuries, for example, formal gardens have featured a

WEATHERING ALL STORMS

Although designed for life in the great outdoors, most garden ornament—new or old—takes a beating when the weather is severe. Moisture, freezing temperatures, acid rain, and road salt are the main culprits, causing clay to crack or flake, wood to rot, and stone to pit, flake, or dissolve away. Even balmy summer air can take its toll, particularly if the humidity is high or you live near the ocean's shore.

Moss adds an aura of age but damages an ornament's surface.

Luckily, most ornament improves with exposure: The grime that shades the fluid garments on a marble statue adds to its appeal, as does the blue-green patina that flowers on antique bronze. Even so, it's important to protect pieces from undue damage and to halt excessive aging before it escalates to complete decay.

The following suggestions will help lengthen your ornament's decorative life.

For starters. Raise all ornament prone to moisture damage up off the ground on a cement, stone, brick, or ceramic footing. Provide good air circulation by pruning back surrounding plants, if possible. Divert sprinklers.

Pots, urns, and vases. Standing water or wet soil will damage cast-iron and stone urns and vases, and can cause any receptacle to crack if it freezes. Check unplanted urns for standing water on a regular basis, and empty them. Likewise, don't plant directly in an ornamental urn. Instead, use it as a cachepot to hold a plastic pot (and drainage saucer), which can be removed when cold weather arrives.

If practical, wheel planted terra-cotta pots under cover (into a greenhouse, potting shed, or garage) when freezing weather approaches, or insulate them well with a blanket of straw held in place with burlap sacking, boards, or netting.

Ornaments carved from soft stone lose detail quickly.

Unwaxed bronze develops a streaked patina over time.

Stone and marble. Any stone that has tiny cracks or absorbs water—such as marble or limestone—is prone to damage from freezing or leaching. But some stones are more vulnerable than others, depending on how soft and porous they are. Newly carved Vicenza limestone, for instance, will begin to lose detail within a decade or two, while antique Portland limestone may take a century or more to show the effects of harsh weather.

Stone and marble ornaments should be shielded from water as much as possible (short of bringing them indoors), but they should not be given any sort of waterproof coating. Each fall, gently brush off excess dirt and grime (which attracts moisture). In cold-weather climates, cover ornaments in winter with a waterproof tarp or custom-made cover like that used on garden furniture, to insulate them from moisture and frost and shield them from airborne particles of road salt. Marble garden ornament, in particular, is best suited to warm climates where the air is dry and freezes rarely occur.

In areas of high humidity, stone ornaments may develop mildew or mold on the side turned away from the sun, or if they're situated in a damp and shady glen. Over a century, this can actually damage the stone, and in the short term, it will stain the surface of the piece. Provide good air circulation if possible. If you find existing mildew unsightly, contact a qualified conservator for treatment recommendations.

High quality cast-stone ornaments are relatively tough, and shouldn't require winter protection.

Bronze. New or old, garden ornaments cast from this copper alloy should be washed once a year during warm weather with mild detergent, water, and a stiff-bristled brush, dried overnight, then waxed with a hard paste wax with a high carnuba content. Never use a spray wax. Apply the wax with a paint brush on a sunny day, let it dry, then buff with a shoe polish brush and cloth to remove any excess. If you want your new bronze to develop a natural patina, leave it unwaxed. If signs of "bronze disease" (powdery spots of light green rather than an overall patina) develop on any bronze ornament, consult a qualified conservator immediately.

Cast iron. To postpone corrosion on new cast-iron ornaments, coat them completely with alkyd enamel paint (or an appropriate primer), acrylic resin formulated for use on metal, cast-iron paint used in automotive restoration work, or hard paste wax with a high carnuba content. The key is to exclude rust-causing moisture before setting cast iron out in the garden.

Note: Some modern sculptures are made with steel that's formulated to rust immediately, then stop. The rust itself provides a protective patina. Such pieces should *not* be painted.

Old cast-iron ornaments inevitably will exhibit previous moisture damage in the form of layers of peeling paint or a veil of rust. If it's the ornament's aura of age you most enjoy, then don't try to restore its original pristine painted finish; you won't like it when your nineteenth-century cast-iron lion looks like it just emerged from the mold. Instead, enjoy it as it is, letting time and weather continue to take their toll. Or seek to preserve the evidence of age (and hence the ornament's character and antique value) while stabilizing the material so the pace of damage slows.

On lightly corroded ornaments, gently clean away as much rust as possible using fine steel wool and lightweight lubricating oil or mineral spirits. Apply acrylic resin or a hard-paste wax with a high carnuba content. If the object in question is fairly new, and you don't mind a painted finish, stabilize it with a rust-converting product such as Rust-Oleum spray enamel paint, available at home centers and hardware stores.

To preserve heavily corroded iron pieces, particularly those with many layers of old paint, consult a qualified conservator.

Lead. Antique lead statues shed water like a tin roof, unless there's a crack in their metal skin. Then moisture can seep in, rust the metal armature inside, and cause it to expand, damaging the piece from within. Have cracks in lead pieces repaired by a qualified conservator. If your antique lead statue retains signs of its original paint that you wish to preserve, consult a professional.

With time, new lead ornaments will develop an attractive white-streaked patina that doesn't need a protective wax or acrylic resin coating. Do, however, shield lead statues from severe winds; blowing sand and grit can abrade them.

Wood. To extend the life of a wooden planter, paint the wood or treat outside surfaces with wood preservative before filling the planter with soil. To avoid damage from within, coat the interior with asphalt emulsion (a roofing product), line the planter with heavy-weight plastic, or fit it with a galvanized metal liner. Be sure to provide for drainage. Carved wood figures also may be treated with preservative, but often look best if left to weather.

A final note: If you're going to enjoy your ornament out in the garden where it belongs (rather than in a protected, indoor environment), some wear and tear is inevitable. In nature, things come and go, from the tiniest plant to the mightiest mountain. Most gardeners wouldn't want it any other way.

For a referral to qualified conservators in your area, write to the American Institute for Conservation of Historic and Artistic Works (AIC), 1717 K St. NW, Suite 301, Washington, DC 20006; phone 202-452-9545; fax 202-452-9328; e-mail infoaic-@aol.com. For additional information about caring for outdoor sculpture, contact Save Outdoor Sculpture (SOS), National Institute for the Conservation of Cultural Property, 3299 K St. NW, Suite 403, Washington, DC 20007.

Some gardeners surrender to the rust on iron pieces.

Cracks in lead pieces cause their hidden structure to rust.

Wood pieces grow more charming with age but soon decay.

quartet of statues that personify the four seasons. Limestone maidens or cast-stone children bearing baskets of flowers or sheaves of wheat paid homage, respectively, to the promise of spring and the bounty of summer; those that bore clusters of grapes or clutched a cloak about their shoulders marked autumn's harvest and the barren months of winter. They often were set in the garden where each would resonate with symbolic meaning: spring in a bed of bulbs, summer near the perennial border, fall beneath the bright-berried viburnum, winter in a clearing amid snow-catching cypress and yew. Many ornament makers still reproduce these four-season figures in stone, lead, cast stone, or concrete, allowing today's gardeners to continue a venerated tradition.

And there are other means to highlight nature's inconstant ways. Look for ornaments—and settings—that will play off one another during the off-season. A giant acorn, for instance, cast from stone and set at the edge of a flower border, may go unnoticed at summer's peak. But when the cosmos goes to seed and the sedum darkens from pink to copper, that acorn will strengthen fall's theme of slow decline and bountiful harvest. A doe and stag, woven from wicker or cast in bronze, may be lost in a garden thicket until December. But when the undergrowth dies back, the figures are unveiled, bringing life to the snowbound scene and compensating for winter's losses. And a cast-stone hare may be forlorn in February, buried nose deep in snow. But when spring arrives, and hoop-petticoat daffodils unfurl around him, that hare will embody the renewal of the season.

The following ornaments will be at home in the garden when summer reigns but take on added meaning during the indicated times of year.

Traditional statues of the four seasons have been popular in gardens for centuries. Here, a sheaf of wheat guarded by a comely maiden symbolizes summer's bounty.

Garlands or baskets of flowers, carried by children or young women, glorified the rebirth of the garden in the spring.

Bronze herons take on a melancholy air against a backdrop of autumn leaves. Soon, the pond in which they fish will be glazed with ice.

This flat carved stone (above) serves up a collection of fall leaves and highlights the season's inevitable decline.

The patina on a bronze stag stands out against an autumn backdrop. His pose suggests caution, as if the scent of humans is in the air.

Autumn

• Large wicker or grapevine baskets set around the garden evoke fall's harvest and also come in handy for collecting spent annuals and other garden debris.

• A broken statue, fractured pillar, or weathered antique wheelbarrow—or any object in a picturesque state of decay or ruin—magnifies the season's sense of nostalgia and decline.

• Boulders, rocks, limestone plinths, statues, and urns that grow a crop of saffron-colored lichen echo the earthy colors of autumn.

• A flying-goose weather vane or whirligig, set on a fence post or the roof of the potting shed, brings to mind the cold-weather migration of real-life flocks, while painted cutouts of Canada geese stand in for the birds that glean fall's just-cut fields.

• Ornaments with design themes of grapes, nuts, squirrels, or twigs celebrate fall's pared-down beauty.

Winter

• Cast-stone finials, grapevine wreaths, wicker figures, rough granite boulders, wattle edgings, piles of rocks, and twig balls catch even the merest dusting of snow, bringing heightened texture to the winter garden.

• A Japanese snow-viewing lantern with a flat cap, or a statue of St. Francis with outstretched arms, will capture more snowfall than an upright obelisk; each ornament's horizontal parts also are apt to spawn a fringe of sparkling icicles as the snow begins to melt.

• The darker the ornament, the more it stands out against a snowy backdrop; lead, bronze, and black granite are better winter choices than marble or limestone.

• Lead urns or frost-proof terra-cotta pots filled with branches of bittersweet (*Celastrus* spp.) or winterberry (*Ilex verticillata*) are

Winter's mantle wraps the shoulders of this statue, while arching branches form a canopy of white. Such horizontal surfaces catch snowfall best.

While the garden sleeps, visiting birds (below) lend their vitality and cheerful demeanor to a chilly scene.

Spiderwebs, invisible on warmer days, stand out like the weavings of winter itself when frost makes a morning visit.

Whether in swollen streams or falling from the sky, the rush of water awakens the land from winter slumber and ushers in the spring. Here, sheets of water pour from the lip of a fountain, hinting at the power of the mountain snowmelt.

A youthful figure of a piper dances in a flower bed bright with the colors of spring. Such exuberance and energy fits the surging nature of the season, when everything seems fresh and newly seen.

White blooms and ornaments will stand out, ghostlike, in the mist or moonlight (opposite).

brilliant beacons in the monochromatic landscape, as are brightly glazed stoneware pots or jars (leave them empty until the spring).

Spring

• Smooth rocks that glisten or deepen in color when washed by rain stand out against spring's first flush of growth.

• Cast-stone figures of birds, rabbits, and baby animals symbolize spring's fecundity; use these sparingly and place them in secret, sheltered spots. Egg-shaped stones, gathered from mountaintop or lakeshore, also are emblems of fertility.

• Bright green and white glazed pots or jars emphasize the freshness of the season.

• Pots sown with winter rye provide eye-catching pools of pure spring green early in the season (and are a great hiding spot for

Easter eggs); add the grass to the compost pile when it's time to fill the pots with summer annuals.

• Marble statues of children, putti, cherubs, or lambs call forth spring's traditional association with youth and rebirth.

In the Night Garden

There's another season of the garden year, often overlooked: a peaceful interval comprising twilight and the darkness just beyond. It is then that the garden seduces us with the scents of night-blooming stock and datura, lemon lilies and nicotiana, traveling on the cooling air. Spades, hoes, rakes, and forks are locked in the potting shed for the night; this is a season for savoring rather than laboring.

The moon rises over the garden, a silver salver on a velvet sky, turning beds and borders into artful compositions of dark and light. Parts of the garden recede and are lost to view, while others emerge from daytime anonymity and take on unaccustomed

Night Lights

Garden night lights can be as ephemeral as a candle glimmering in a paper lantern, or as fleeting as a fountain of fireworks set off like Vesuvius in a cast-iron urn. But for more lasting pleasures, install permanent fixtures to light up your garden's ornament.

Effective lighting techniques include spotlighting (a strong beam of light that illuminates a statue or sculpture from afar), back lighting (a soft light placed behind an ornament that creates a silhouette rimmed by light), skim lighting (a broad-beamed light, placed close by an ornament and to its side, that skims over its surface and highlights its texture), and area lighting (a soft, diffused light that illuminates a small garden area and the ornament it contains).

While you're planning your garden lighting scheme, on your own or with help from a lighting designer, don't overlook the possibilities for creating garden ornament with

continued on page 106

continued from page 105

artificial lighting. Use lights to cast shadows and create patterns and forms that don't exist in the light of day: the lacy leafwork of nandina writ large upon the garden wall, or the uplit trunks and branches of a spreading oak, decidedly sculptural against the starry night sky.

Light fixtures themselves can also bring beauty and artistry to the garden. Increasingly, utilitarian safety lighting designed to illuminate steps and pathways is being transformed into small-scale metal sculpture, often in the shape of copper-capped mushrooms.

A final note: Subtlety is a virtue unless your garden is of a theatrical bent. Use low-wattage lights where possible, and place others on a dimmer. The challenge is to highlight the darkness, with all its magic and mystery, not to recreate the brilliance of day.

Vintage Japanese lanterns glow softly in the waning light and are as fragile and emphemeral as the garden's finest flowers.

prominence. The Shasta daisies. The quartz pebbles and creamy shells embedded in the walkway. The white stripes on a trio of pots. The marble bust at the end of the path. The artemisia and ribbon grass. The moon works its alchemy and turns them all to platinum, as striking as any iris or dahlia in the revealing light of day. Their lack of color is the key: any ornament or plant that is white, off white, silver, or variegated with white will stand out like a candle in a coal mine once the sun goes down.

But moonlight and alba roses will take you only so far. If you plan to serve dinner under the stars or dance on the patio till dawn, you'll need to supplement the lunar light.

There's a long tradition of using candles and oil lamps to ornament and illuminate the nighttime garden. During the sixteenth century, flames flickered in special niches behind waterfalls in India's finest Moghul gardens. In Ottoman Turkey during the early eighteenth century, tortoises with small lamps attached to their shells meandered along the paths of the Sultan's garden

during the tulip festival, held each April during the full moon. Later that same century, London's Vauxhall Gardens glittered at night with more than a thousand glass lamps hung from the branches of trees, rendering the pleasure grounds "exceedingly light and brilliant," according to one observer.

In this country, from the 1890s through the 1920s, paper lanterns imported from Japan filled nighttime gardens with a romantic glow conducive to festive garden parties and celebrations of the Fourth of July. Their brilliant beauty—a multitude of colored moons floating in the night—was a favorite subject of painters such as Childe Hassam, and created memories of enchanted evenings that lasted a lifetime.

Today, there are many ways to make the garden sparkle after dark. Some are based on long tradition; paper Japanese lanterns still enchant, as do tiki torches, or luminarias made from paper bags and set along a garden path. Japanese lanterns carved from stone are a more permanent addition. Although often used for the interest of their form alone, stone lanterns should be placed where they make functional sense, such as at the junction of two pathways.

Other ornamental garden lights are new interpretations of old designs. There are so-called beehive lanterns, in the shape of old-fashioned terra-cotta forcers, which cast dancing rays of light. There are glass-and-iron hurricane lanterns, a wealth of candle lanterns and votive holders on stakes, and hanging lanterns in a variety of styles, some akin to Vauxhall's famous lights.

Such gleaming ornaments introduce us to an altered garden, where little is familiar and much is newly seen. We linger there, listening to the crickets and counting the stars, until the last flame fades.

Delicate paper lanterns have lent their festive air to the evening garden for more than a century. Candles are their traditional light source, but lanterns also can be fitted with small electric bulbs.

Judiciously chosen and carefully placed, lights transform a garden's character once the sun disappears.

LAYING CLAIM: MAKING THE GARDEN YOURS

FOR SOME GARDENERS, THERE COMES a day when conventional ornament alone fails to satisfy. It is then that we look for new ways to make our mark and bring individuality, creativity, and emotional meaning to the garden.

We salvage rocks that once lined our grandparents' flower beds and nestle them around our plots of penstemon and lavender. We set out concrete stepping-stones marked with handprints of our kids, or hang up out-of-tune windbells they made at camp or school. We add our own quirky or artistic touches: chunky wooden plant stakes painted robin's-egg blue, a druid's circle of golden gazing globes among the ornamental grasses, or a pot encrusted with bits of colored china—the treasured remains of a broken heirloom plate.

Such ornaments are personal rather than blandly generic, surprising rather than predictable. Some are rich with sentiment or

A wooden figure, crowned with leaves and bright as a painted bunting, reigns as queen of this New Mexico garden.

*B*robdingnagian dragonflies and butterflies (opposite) give this garden a fantastic air. A wicker tunnel—or is that a caterpillar?—wiggles through the background.

Cobalt-blue blossoms burst forth on this leafless tree, which seems to have expensive taste in water.

A stone metate collected on long-ago travels serves as a memorable finial at the corner of this garden wall.

memory, others rife with humor. Still others are irreverent, turning tradition on its head, or daringly artistic. All are pieces of ourselves and our lives that we plant in the garden—our way of laying claim to the land.

Keepers of Memory

Perhaps a green-painted watering can conjures up memories of your dad, who wielded it to water his seedlings for more than fifty years; set it in the garden in a place of honor. Maybe a glazed jardinière, bursting with purple pansies, brings to mind the aunt who first introduced you to these clown-faced blooms; place it on the deck where you'll see it while you drink your morning coffee. Like photo albums, ornaments like these have the power to evoke the people you love along with the places you've visited. They prompt you to venture down forgotten pathways. And as you hoe in the hush of morning, or kneel in the cedar mulch to plant a new geranium, a cavalcade of images keeps you company.

Although their significance may go unrecognized by garden visitors, the following types of ornament bestow the richness of memory on many a garden.

Mementos. Souvenirs of adventures far from home fit naturally into the garden's beds. Shells collected on a Caribbean beach at low tide, oval stones as smooth as soap gathered on the shores of the Great Lakes, a carving of a coyote brought back from Santa Fe, or a brightly glazed pot packed home from Portugal all revive special moments for the gardener.

Remembrances. Gifts from other gardeners, from your friends, or from your kids, or belongings from a special person or the past (the birdbath from your mother's garden, or the stone turtle you used as a horse at the age of four), all serve to bring a person or time of life to mind. Some gardeners even include a remembrance marker in a contemplative garden spot: a small stone, marble slab, or brass plaque marked with the name or initials of a beloved parent, spouse, child, or friend.

Quirky folk art, brought home to the garden from foreign lands, recalls good times and adventures.

Markers in a quiet garden spot (above) evoke memories and invite introspection.

Each ornament, pot, pipe, and plant here has a story.

MEMORIES *in* MOSAIC

Pots, stepping-stones, or patios encrusted with bits of broken china and other mementos are the patchwork quilts of the garden: durable, practical, and bright with pieces of the past. Sometimes known as *piqué assiette,* or memory ware, these garden ornaments are part of a tradition of mosaic art that stretches back to ancient Greece, where artists pressed colored pebbles into mortar.

*O*ld bricks, broken pavers, and a collection of special tiles blend together to form a colorful pathway into the past.

The key to assembling colorful garden mosaics is thinking ahead. Every time you drop and break a plate or coffee mug, save it in a box for future projects. (Breaking fine antique plates on purpose is cheating.) When you're out scouring local estate sales, hoping to find that perfect corner cupboard, keep an eye out for chipped or cracked china that can be yours for a quarter. Collect leftover tiles from your neighbor's kitchen remodeling, marbles from your son or daughter, and discontinued samples from your local tile store. And on trips abroad, seek out inexpensive tiles that capture the style of a region.

For a patio project, use some of the objects whole or break them into smaller pieces. Wrap plates or tiles in a towel and break them with a hammer, or into small pieces with tile nippers. Be sure to wear gloves and safety goggles.

For best effect, lay most of the patio with plain bricks, flagstones, or ceramic pavers, filling only small, odd-shaped areas with mosaic. Set broken tile and plate shards into mortar and let dry, then grout just as you would with any outdoor tile. File or sand down any sharp edges to protect bare feet.

Reserve marbles for spots that won't get much traffic, and save pieces such as cup handles or teapot spouts for vertical surfaces.

Use an adaptation of this basic technique to make mosaic-covered pots or stepping-stones. You'll need the following:

- Terra-cotta pot or concrete stepping-stone;
- Supply of cracked or broken plates, cups, tiles, buttons, coins, beads, and other small mementos (the quirkier the better);
- Waterproof adhesive, such as ceramic wall-tile adhesive or concrete bonding adhesive;
- Hammer or tile nippers;
- Safety goggles;
- Sanded tile grout (gray is a good starter color);
- Sponge;
- Sandpaper, file, or sanding block;
- Penetrating grout sealer.

With waterproof adhesive, glue shards to the pot or stepping-stone in the desired pattern and let dry overnight. Mix grout according to package directions and press carefully and liberally into spaces between shards. (Shard edges are sharp—use extreme caution.) Wipe off excess grout with a damp sponge. When the grout is dry, file or sand down the sharp edges. Coat the object with penetrating sealer (follow manufacturer's directions).

Marbles accent a composition of broken tiles.

Colorful mosaic-work brightens a garden corner.

An orderly array of tiles suits some gardeners best.

This quirky wall is studded with shells and crockery.

Gray and white stones form a striking sunburst.

Tiny bits of tile camouflage an ordinary garden pot.

Sun-bleached crab claws, necklaces of shells, and other marine mementos bring the sound of the sea to this landlocked garden corner.

A weathered cross (right) and a pair of tin milagros, tacked to a rustic gate, commemorate a miracle and intensify the earthy spirituality of this garden spot.

A beloved English bulldog merited this garden marker; another cherished canine, Winnie Darling, lies nearby.

Memorials. When Queen Victoria's favorite greyhound, Eos, died in 1844, she commissioned a bronze likeness of the dog and had it erected in the garden. Such monuments, dedicated to a cherished canine, were common in Victorian times and often boasted lengthy tributes to the dog's courage and fidelity. Few gardeners today have Queen Victoria's means, but many make a place among the peonies and bleeding hearts for simple markers bearing the names of honored family pets.

Commemoratives. In many Latin American countries and in New Mexico, families hang up embossed metal plaques or objects, called *milagros,* to commemorate a miracle, to give thanks for a blessing, or as votive offerings to the saints. Most *milagros* are made of tin, cut in the shape of body parts such as eyes, arms, hearts, or hands. Such reminders of life's blessings are a rich addition to the garden, whether to mark a birth, healing, marriage, or other joyous event, or simply to give thanks for strong legs, clear eyesight, or breaths of fresh air.

Wit and Artistry

Ornaments that evoke memory provide intensely private pleasures. Witty or inventive ornaments, on the other hand, are meant to be shared. Through them, gardeners willingly reveal themselves: their creativity, their sense of humor, their idiosyncrasies, their desire to make a garden unlike any other. When we stumble across such ornaments in a garden, they pique our curiosity, and we remember them long after visions of flowers and shrubbery fade.

"What made them think of that?" we wonder. What inner muse made one gardener hang teacups from a tree like Christmas ornaments, set baseballs on tree limbs like a crop of albino oranges, or plant plates in the yard as if they were exotic succulents from another planet? What prompted another to surround a birdbath with a carpet of cat's-eye marbles, drape faux pearls around the neck of a virginal statue, or erect a pregnant scarecrow to watch over the pumpkin patch? What urged yet another

Hide and Seek

Keep some ornament in hiding, for your eyes only. Tuck a pair of ceramic toads under the low hanging leaves of the ligularia. Set a brass heart in the baby's tears, where you'll see it when you weed. Scatter some glass beads in a frequently turned bed, and enjoy the luster of buried treasure when you plant. Position a statue in a nook behind the potting shed, where only you will visit. All will bring secret pleasure while you go about your garden labors.

Mona Lisa smiles add an aura of serenity to these enigmatic heads, carved from rounded stones and left to lie in the garden. Easily overlooked, they promote a thrilling sense of discovery when stumbled upon during garden explorations.

GUARDIANS *of* the GARDEN

Scarecrow may be a misnomer for this garden guardian.

A
ll gardeners, no matter how tireless, need a stand-in in the garden to watch over the hills of newly planted corn or to guard the tasty tendrils of the first sweet peas. So get out the rag bag. Pull out your safety pins, paints, and cast-off shoes, and revive your sense of humor. A scarecrow can be defending your crops—and providing comic relief in the garden—by sundown.

Framework. To form the scarecrow's backbone, choose a sturdy pole or stick 6 to 7 feet in length. Lash a shorter stick (4 to 5 feet long) to the backbone for the arms. At this point, you can either pound the long pole into the ground where you want your scarecrow to stand and assemble the scarecrow on it, or assemble the scarecrow on the framework and then put it in place. Once it's up, don't worry if the arms aren't quite parallel to the ground; sometimes a jaunty angle looks best.

Body building. For the scarecrow's torso, fill an old pillowcase with straw (for tradition's sake) or with plastic-foam packing peanuts. Tie the case closed, then tie it to the backbone where the arms are attached and let it hang down in front.

Dress-up. Slip a tattered flannel shirt over the arms and button it over the torso. Stuff the sleeves with straw, or let them hang loose. Old denim jeans or overalls come next. If you're assembling the scarecrow before putting up the framework, slip the upright pole through one of the scarecrow's pants legs. Stuff the pants if you like; just be sure to tie them closed at the cuffs so the straw or plastic foam

A rumpled professor oversees labors of the garden.

Even an urban garden needs a scarecrow, if only for show.

peanuts don't escape. Buckle the overalls over the scarecrow's shoulders, or pin the pants to the shirt or torso (add a rope through the belt loops for a belt). Next, add old garden gloves (stuffed, of course) and discarded boots or shoes.

Getting a head. A round pillow, small pillow case (stuffed), small burlap sack (stuffed), dried gourd, or upside-down pail all make suitable heads. Give the scarecrow a face with acrylic paints or permanent markers, then use wire or twine to secure the head to the pole (or place the pail over the end of the pole). The final touch? A tattered straw hat and a weathered rake or hoe so the scarecrow can get to work.

Breaking with tradition. Don't feel your scarecrow has to fit the traditional mold. Get inspiration from what you have on hand: a cast-off maternity dress, a holey pair of fishing waders, an old flannel nightgown or pair of pajamas. Build a body from terra-cotta pots, stove pipe, or pieces of driftwood. Make a monk for your medieval herb garden or a bee keeper for your hives. They may not scare a wise old crow, but they'll bring a light-hearted touch to all your work.

Arms askew, this scarecrow has an "I dare you" air.

This artsy figure performs a primitive garden rite.

Dapper formality is this scarecrow's strategy.

No solitary duty for this scarecrow pair.

Sheer bulk gives this scarecorw madam an advantage in the ongoing battle of the birds.

*B*rilliant glass flowers wave
above real-life blooms, their
sensuous forms an artist's
tribute to the glories of the
garden.

A sophisticated figure loses its
hauteur when its neck and
arms sprout weeds and flowers.

to upholster a garden chair with a seat of turf, or paint an urn-on-plinth a shocking blue? The answers may evade us, but no matter: a lasting impression has been made.

Expressing your own particular brand of humor, artistry, or quirky taste in the garden may take practice; many of us lost faith in our creative abilities sometime around the fifth grade. The following ways of thinking about ornament may help launch you on your way.

Tweaking tradition Take a traditional garden ornament and give it a twist by placing it in an unexpected position, making it from an unexpected material, or painting it an unexpected color. Cut out shapes from plywood and paint them to mimic formal urns, obelisks, or classical columns. Form bed edgings from colored bottles or thrift-store plates rather than from bricks. Paint your bean poles purple or plant a pot with stones. Dare to be different.

Out of place. Enlist objects from other spheres of life to stand in as garden ornament: a mannequin to mimic a statue, a vintage standing lamp to support a vine, a child's pedal car to hold a wealth of potted plants, a dollar's worth of pennies to glimmer in the paving. Or show your ingenuity by recycling old bed springs into trellises for your snap peas, by turning galvanized trash-can lids into birdbaths, by transforming an antique china wash basin into a gurgling fountain, or by building a figure worthy of *The Wizard of Oz* out of funnels and sieves and oddball pots and pans.

Funky garage-sale plates on wooden stems stand in for garden flowers in this irreverent scheme.

Painted plywood and plastic columns (above) stand in for relics of the classical age.

A shimmering circle of gazing globes (left) conjures up images of hot-air balloon ascensions or alien landings, depending on your leanings.

Risk Free

When it comes to working with garden ornament, there are guidelines galore, established by generations of garden makers. *Keep it simple. Stick to one theme. Don't mix styles. Avoid wholesale copying.* But this last is the wisest: *Don't be afraid to experiment.*

Many garden ornaments are easy to move and can be added, subtracted, or repositioned on a whim. So play around. See what you like. There's nothing to lose and much to gain. You may have just the knack for combining a flock of whirligigs with a life-size cutout of a Jersey cow, or for melding awning-striped pots with a classical statue of Apollo. You'll never know unless you try.

Remember, too, that what delights your eye this season or this year may fade in appeal with familiarity—in fact, you may stop seeing certain ornaments altogether as time goes by. Simply placing that stone orb or pot in a new position in the garden will resurrect its power to please.

Near to life. Catch the eye with look-alikes. Position a bronze duck with outspread wings over the garden pond, as if on course for landing. Sink a cast-stone hippo into the lawn, as if he's basking in a jungle pool. Place a folk art heron alongside a dry streambed of river rock, and tempt him with a cut-tin ornament of a jumping trout. Situate a carving of a giant peach beneath a tree in the orchard, or a foot-high acorn beneath an aged oak.

Tongue in cheek. Have fun with familiar themes. Twine a rubber serpent around the trunk of the apple tree, or secure a fig leaf or breechclout on a classical statue. Dress a scarecrow in a cast-off tuxedo, or suspend a grinning Cheshire cat mask from the branch of a tree. Cater to childhood fantasies and sink a boat in a garden pond so that only the rigging shows, like a shipwreck off an uncharted isle.

A gardener's undying passion for gnomes and brilliant hues is manifest in this Irish garden, where a sense of play prevails.

Kitsch as kitsch can. Don't be afraid to buck the tides of taste. If pink flamingos remind you of the neighbor lady who supplied you with contraband cookies as a child, by all means, import some to your patch of lawn. If iron-clad wagon wheels among your cacti transport you to the Old West, roll them in and dream away. And if gold pots and statuary makes you feel like the czar before the Revolution, let the gilding begin.

As you seek to make your mark, you may raise eyebrows—of the postman, of the neighbors, of your mother. Yet your garden is yours to do with as you will; it is your arena, your sketch pad, your canvas—your place to experiment and discover what you like or to express the self you have already come to know.

So give your imagination—and your heart—free reign. Make way for whim and fancy. Listen to your inner voices and quell your inner critic. Go outside and play.

Balanced on clay-pipe pedestals, bowling balls stand in for classic stone orbs and mimic the shapes of barrel cacti.

Metal leaves sprout from an exuberant ceramic pot (opposite), causing double takes in this romantic garden clearing.

THE THINGS WE LOVE

WHEN ALL IS SAID AND done, making ourselves at home in the garden may involve nothing more than including a smattering of objects we love among the plants we cherish. What those objects are and how we find them will vary widely, according to the gardener.

Some gardeners are tied to tradition and formality; for them, classical statues, urns, and fountains will provide the richness of history, dignified tone, and familiarity they seek. Treasure hunters without par, they'll scour high-end antique shops at home and abroad, track down traditional manufacturers, and pore over auction and mail-order catalogs until they unearth the perfect marble wood nymph, cast-iron lion, or Portland-stone urn.

Some gardeners have an undying affinity for rocks; for them the weight and substance of boulder, stone, or fossil will attract with near magnetic force. They'll cart home river stones from mountain journeys, jam on the brakes to scoop storm-tumbled

This shapely cap secures plant stakes in a tepee and guards the gardener from their pointed ends.

A trough for alpine plants (opposite) brings a bit of beloved mountain flora into this dooryard. These specialized containers once were made from old stone troughs or sinks; now most are formed from hypertufa —a mix of cement, sand, and peat moss.

Marble hands, clasped in friendship, distill the amicable spirit of gardening into sculpted form.

rocks from the roadway, or hire the neighbor with the backhoe to unearth a boulder, embedded with ancient seashells, from a nearby field.

For other gardeners, the lure will be garden gnomes, produced in Germany as early as the eighteenth century; painted figures of cows and pigs; a subdivision's worth of whimsical birdhouses; or 1940s one-dimensional yard art of plump ladies weeding and showing off their bloomers. Garage sales, thrift stores, country antique shops, roadside vendors, and jam-packed basements and attics will constitute their hunting grounds.

Still others will be drawn to ornaments garnered from garden shops and nurseries, or made to order, such as the simplest of terra-cotta pots, or stones engraved with quotes from William Shakespeare, Emily Dickinson, John Lennon, or the Bible. All of us have our own objects of affection.

What matters most is that the ornament in your garden means something to *you*. That it quickens your heart and elicits your laughter. That seeing it tucked among the alstroemeria or entangled in sweet peas makes you remember, think, dream, and feel. And that when you go to the garden, in the brightness of morning or the evening's last light, you find a deep and lasting pleasure.

SOURCE
GUIDE

GENERAL GARDEN ORNAMENT

From AESTHETICA

From CAPE COD CUPOLA

AESTHETICA
P.O. Box 14
Gilbertsville, NY 13776
607 · 783 · 2114
♦ *Garden ironwork, gates and tables.*

AMERICAN ORNAMENT STUDIO, INC.
712 Bryant St.
San Francisco, CA 94107
415 · 543 · 1363
♦ *Fountains, stepping stones, animals, benches and pedestals.*

AMERICAN SUNDIALS, INC.
P.O. Box 677
Point Arena, CA 95468
707 · 884 · 3082
♦ *Sand-cast bronze sundials in a variety of styles.*

THE ANTIQUE ROSE EMPORIUM
Route 5, Box 143
Brenham, TX 77833
800 · 441 · 0002
♦ *Rustic cedar garden furniture.*

AUTUMN FORGE
1104 N. Buena Vista Ave.
Orlando, FL 32818
407 · 293 · 3302
♦ *Handmade plant hangers in forged iron, as well as garden dinner bells, racks and sconces.*

BAKER'S LAWN ORNAMENTS
RD5, Box 265
Somerset, PA 15501
814 · 445 · 7028
♦ *Gazing globes in seven colors*

THE BAMBOO FENCER
32 Germania St.
Jamaica Plain, MA 02130
617 · 524 · 6137
♦ *Bamboo garden structures, birdhouses and bamboo poles.*

BOWBENDS
P.O. Box 900
Bolton, MA 01740
508 · 779 · 6464
♦ *Gazebos and other garden structures from arbors and pergolas to small bridges, trellage and follies.*

CAPE COD CUPOLA
78 State Rd.
North Dartmouth, MA 02747-2994
508 · 994 · 2119
♦ *Weather vanes.*

DECORATIVE CRAFTS, INC.
50 Chestnut St.
P.O. Box 4308
Greenwich, CT. 06830
203 · 531 · 1500
♦ *Assorted garden ornament, including Oriental porcelain garden seats.*

DELANEY & COCHRAN
156 South Park
San Francisco, CA 94107
415 · 896 · 2998

(FAX) 415 · 896 · 2995

♦ *Fountains.*

DESIGN TOSCANO, INC.
17 East Campbell St.
Arlington Heights, IL 60005
800 · 525 · 0733

♦ *Cast resin statues, figurines, birdbaths, plaques, gargoyles and other ornament.*

DEVONSHIRE
1 East Washington St.
Middleburg, VA 20118
540 · 687 · 3623

♦ *New and antique garden ornament and furniture. Devonshire also has shops in Carmel, CA, Aspen, CO, Newport, RI, Greenwich, CT, Bridgehampton and Easthampton, NY, Naples and Palm Beach, FL.*

ELIZABETH STREET GARDENS
1176 Second Ave.
New York, NY 10021
212 · 941 · 4800

♦ *Large assortment of statuary, fountains, urns, pedestals and other ornament.*

FLORENTINE CRAFTSMEN, INC.
46-24 28th St.
Long Island City, NY 11101
718 · 937 · 7632

♦ *Handcrafted statuary, planters, urns and fountains.*

FOLLY
13 White St.
New York, NY 10013

212 · 925 · 5012

♦ *Distinctive garden ornaments, including stone griffins, statuary and fountains.*

GARDEN ESCAPE
www.garden.com

♦ *Garden ornament through the Web.*

GARDEN MAGIC
1930 Wake Forest Rd.
Raleigh, NC 27608
919 · 821 · 1997

♦ *Light fixtures, trellises, topiary frames, trogs and sundials.*

THE GARDENER
1836 Fourth St.
Berkeley, CA 94710
510 · 548 · 4545

♦ *Assorted garden ornament and furniture.*

GARDENER'S EDEN
P.O. Box 7307
San Francisco, CA 94120-7307
415 · 421 · 4242

♦ *Assorted garden ornament, furniture, planters, trellises, arbors, lanterns, birdhouses.*

GARDENER'S SUPPLY COMPANY
128 Intervale Rd.
Burlington, VT 05401-2850
800 · 863 · 1700

♦ *Assorted garden ornament.*

GOOD DIRECTIONS
24 Ardmore Rd.
Stamford, CT 06902

From BOWBENDS

From FOLLY

From GARDEN MAGIC

From KINSMAN COMPANY, INC.

From NICHOLS BROTHERS
STONEWORKS

From ROBINSON IRON

800 · 346 · 7678
◆ *Copper and brass weather vanes.*

GRIGGS NURSERY
1021 David Ave.
Pacific Grove, CA 93950
408 · 373 · 4495
and at
9220 Carmel Valley Rd.
Carmel Valley, CA 93923
408 · 626 · 0680
◆ *Garden ornament and large
selection of terra-cotta pots.*

THE GROVE HOMESCAPES
472 Lighthouse Ave.
Pacific Grove, CA 93950
408 · 656 · 0864
◆ *Giant iron sunflowers and other
garden ornament.*

JACKSON & PERKINS
P.O. Box 1028
Medford, OR 97501
800 · 292 · 4769
◆ *Trellises and arbors.*

KENNETH LYNCH & SONS, INC.
84 Danbury Rd.
Wilton, CT 06897
203 · 762 · 8363
◆ *Hugh selection of garden
ornament, from the diminutive
to the monumental.*

KINSMAN COMPANY, INC.
River Rd.
Point Pleasant, PA 18950
800 · 733 · 4146
◆ *Assorted ornament, trellises,
edgings, labels, pots.*

LAZY HILL FARM DESIGNS
P.O. Box 235
Colerain, NC 27924
919 · 356 · 2828
◆ *Copper sculptures, hand-crafted
birdhouses and feeders.*

MARCIA DONAHUE
3017 Wheeler St.
Berkeley, CA 94705
510 · 540 · 8544
◆ *Stone garden sculptures.*

MILAEGER'S GARDENS
4838 Douglas Ave.
Racine, WI 53402-2498
800 · 669 · 9956
◆ *Gazing globes and assorted
garden ornament.*

MISS TRAWICK'S GARDEN SHOP
664 Lighthouse Ave.
Pacific Grove, CA 93950
408 · 375 · 4605
◆ *Rustic trellises, garden furniture
and assorted ornament.*

MUSEUM GIFT SHOP AND
NEW ENGLAND BOOKSTORE
Old Sturbridge Village
1 Old Sturbridge Village Rd.
Sturbridge, MA 01566
◆ *Covered ridge bird feeder kit,
country barn birdhouse kit, glazed
redware flowerpots (replica of
1830s design).*

NEW ENGLAND GARDEN
ORNAMENTS
38 E. Brookfield Rd.
North Brookfield, MA 01535

508 · 867 · 4474
(FAX) 508 · 867 · 8409
♦ *Importers of UK garden ornament, including lead statues, fountains, planters and rose arches.*

NICHOLS BROTHERS
STONEWORKS
20209 Broadway
Snohomish, WA 98290
360 · 668 · 5434
♦ *Dry-cast sandstone urns, pots
and small statues.*

ROBINSON IRON
P.O. Box 1235
Robinson Rd.
Alexander City, AL 35010
205 · 329 · 8486
♦ *Cast-iron garden ornament and
reproduction fountains.*

SEAHORSE TRADING CO., INC.
P.O. Box 677
Berryville, VA 22611
540 · 955 · 1677
♦ *Imported fountains, birdbaths,
lions, wellheads, lead figures.*

SMITH & HAWKEN
117 E. Strawberry Dr.
Mill Valley, CA 94941
415 · 383 · 4415
♦ *Assorted garden ornament, furniture, planters, trellises, arbor
lanterns, birdhouses. Also in retail
stores nationwide.*

STONE FOREST
P.O. Box 2840
Santa Fe, NM 87504

505 · 986 · 8883
♦ *Hand-carved granite spheres,
fountains, bowls, basins, lanterns
and benches.*

SUCCULENT GARDENS & GIFTS
3672 The Barnyard
Carmel, CA
408 · 624 · 0426
♦ *Large assortment of wind chimes,
stepping-stones, bonsai pots and
other ornament.*

WIND & WEATHER
The Alvion St. Water Tower
P.O. Box 2320
Mendocino, CA 95460
800 · 922 · 9463
♦ *Vertical and horizontal sundials,
armillary-sphere sundials, gazing
globes and weather vanes.*

WINTERTHUR MUSEUM &
GARDEN
100 Enterprises Place
Dover, DE 19901
800 · 767 · 0500
♦ *Iron garden furniture, brass
cranes, birdhouses.*

OLD AND ANTIQUE ORNAMENT

AILEEN MINOR AMERICAN
ANTIQUES
30550 Washington St.
P.O. Box 40
Princess Anne, MD 21853

From WIND & WEATHER

From WINTERTHUR MUSEUM
& GARDEN

From BARBARA ISRAEL GARDEN ANTIQUES

410 · 651 · 0075
♦ *Gallery specializing in antique fountains, statuary, benches, statues.*

BARBARA ISRAEL GARDEN ANTIQUES
21 East 79th St.
New York, NY 10021
♦ *Antique garden ornament.*

BUTTERFIELD & BUTTERFIELD
220 San Bruno Ave.
San Francisco, CA 94103
415 · 8 61 · 7500
♦ *Auction house.*

CHRISTIE'S
502 Park Ave.
New York, NY 10021
212 · 546 · 1000
(FAX) 212 · 588 · 1530
♦ *Auction house*

CHRISTOPHER FILLEY ANTIQUES
1707 West 45th St.
Kansas City, MO 64112
816 · 561 · 1124
♦ *Old and antique fountains, statuary, urns.*

GARDEN ACCENTS
947 Longview Rd.
Gulph Mills, PA 19406
610 · 825 · 5525
♦ *Antique garden ornament, including urns, planters, statues, fountains.*

GARDEN PARK ANTIQUES
515 West Thompson Lane
Nashville, TN 37211

615 · 254 · 1996
♦ *Garden and architectural antiques.*

GARTH'S AUCTION INC.
2690 Stratford Rd.
P.O. Box 369
Delaware, OH 43015
614 · 362 · 4771
♦ *Auction house.*

H. CROWTHER LTD.
5 High Road
Chesiwick, London W4 2ND
011 · 44 · 1819 · 442326
♦ *Auction house.*

LINDA PEARCE ANTIQUES
1214 West 47th St.
Kansas City, MO 64112
816 · 531 · 6255
♦ *Old and antique fountains, statuary, architectural items, urns, planters.*

THE MARSTON HOUSE
Main Street
Wiscasset, ME 04578
207 · 882 · 6010
♦ *Antique English and New England garden ornament.*

MARSTON LUCE
1314 21st St. NW
Washington, DC 20036
202 · 775 · 9460
♦ *Old and antique garden furniture, urns, fountains, statuary.*

SOTHEBY'S
1334 York Ave.

New York, NY 10021
212 · 606 · 7000
♦ *Auction house.*

TANCREDI & MORGEN
7174 Carmel Valley Rd.
Carmel, CA 93923
408 · 625 · 4477
♦ *Antique garden ornament and old English pots.*

TREILLAGE
418 East 75th St.
New York, NY 10021
212 · 535 · 2288
(FAX) 212 · 517 · 6589
♦ *Antique garden ornament.*

TRENT ANTIQUES
3729 South Drive Highway
West Palm Beach, FL 33405
561 · 832 · 0919
♦ *Period pieces only.*

WHITEHALL AT THE VILLA
1213 E. Franklin St.
Chapel Hill, NC 27514
919 · 942 · 3179
♦ *Antique fountains, statuary and benches.*

WICKETS GARDEN STYLE
17 South Madison St.
Middleburg, VA 20118
800 · 585 · 1225
♦ *Antique ornaments, pots and forcers.*

POTS AND CONTAINERS

BRANDON INDUSTRIES, INC.
4419 Westgrove Dr.
Dallas, TX 75245
972 · 529 · 6000
♦ *Cast aluminum planters and urns.*

CLAYCRAFT
807 Avenue of the Americas
New York, NY 10001
212 · 242 · 2903
♦ *Fiberglass planters.*

INTERNATIONAL BONSAI
ARBORETUM
P.O. Box 23894
Rochester, NY 14692
716 · 334 · 2595
♦ *Bonsai containers and trays.*

PEMBRIDGE TERRACOTTA
Victoria Place
Leominster
Hereford, HR6 9HB
United Kingdom
011 · 44 · 1544 · 388696
pembridgeterracotta@btinternet.com
♦ *English handthrown terra-cotta pots, jars and forcers, including custom-made commemorative pots.*

WHICHFORD POTTERY
Shipston-on-Stour
Warwickshire
CV36 5PG
011 · 44 · 1608 · 684416
♦ *English terra-cotta pots.*

From CLAYCRAFT

From INTERNATIONAL BONSAI ARBORETUM

From VIXEN HILL

STRUCTURES

AMDEGA MACHIN DESIGNS
557 Danbury Rd.
Wilton, CT 06897
800 · 622 · 4464
♦ *English garden pavilions, summerhouses, conservatories.*

STICKNEY'S GARDEN HOUSE &
FOLLIES
One Thompson Square
P.O. Box 34
Boston, MA 02129
617 · 242 · 1711
♦ *Wood garden pavilions, follies and temples.*

VINTAGE WOODWORKS
Highway 34S, P.O. Box R
Quinlan, TX 75474
903 · 356 · 2158
♦ *Garden gazebos.*

VIXEN HILL
Main St.
Elverson, PA 19520
800 · 423 · 2760
♦ *Garden gazebos.*

THE BIRDS
AND
THE BEES

COLONIAL WILLIAMSBURG
P.O. Box CH
Williamsburg, VA 23187
757 · 220 · 7286
♦ *Redware bird bottles, garden bench, sundial.*

CONSUMER INFORMATION CENTER – 40
P.O. Box 100
Pueblo, CO 81002
719 · 948 · 3334
♦ *Request the "For the Birds" brochure packet.*

DUNCRAFT
102 Fisherville Rd.
Concord, OH 03303-2086
800 · 593 · 5656
♦ *Birdhouses and bird feeders.*

ENTOMO-LOGIC
9807 NE 140th St.
Bothell, WA 98011-5132
425 · 820 · 8037
easugdenamsn.com
♦ *Mason bee supplies and educational information.*

HYDE BIRDFEEDER CO.
56 Felton St.
P.O. Box 168
Waltham, MA 02254
♦ *Bird feeders in many styles.*

KNOX CELLARS NATIVE
POLLINATORS
1607 Knox Ave.
Bellingham, WA 98225
360 · 733 · 3283
knoxclr@accessone.com
Website:
www.accessone.com/~knoxclr
♦ *Assorted mason bee nesting blocks, video and audio tapes on mason bees, bumble bee houses,*

nesting material for ceretina bees.

WILD BIRD SUPPLIES
4815 Oak St.
Crystal Lake, IL 60012
815 · 455 · 4020
♦ *Large assortment of birdhouses and feeders.*

LIGHTING

COPPER CRAFT LIGHTING, INC.
5100-1BC Clayton Rd.
Suite 291
Concord, CA 94521
510 · 672 · 4337

DONER DESIGN
2175 Beaver Valley Pike
New Providence, PA 17560
717 · 786 · 8891
♦ *Copper garden lights.*

JOSIAH R. COPPERSMYTHE
80 Stiles Rd.
Boylston, MA 01505
800 · 426 · 8249
♦ *Brass or copper outdoor lanterns.*

OTHER RESOURCES

AMERICAN INSTITUTE FOR CONSERVATION OF HISTORIC AND ARTISTIC WORKS (AIC)
1717 K. St. NW
Suite 301
Washington, DC 20006
202 · 452 · 9545

E-mail: Infoaic@aol.com
♦ *Recommendations for qualified conservators.*

CONSERVATOR'S EMPORIUM
100 Standing Rock Circle
Reno, NV 89511
702 · 852 · 0404
♦ *Conservation supplies such as Carnuba Wax #1, Rennaisance Wax and the acrylic resin Acryloid B-48N. Minimum $25 order.*

NORTH AMERICAN SUNDIAL SOCIETY
8 Sachem Dr.
Glastonburg, CT 06033
860 · 633 · 8655
♦ *Publishes a journal on sundials four times a year.*

SARA SCHECHNER GENUTH
Gnomon Research
Customized Curatorial Services
1142 Loxford Terrace
Silver Spring, MD 20901
301 · 593 · 2626
♦ *Curatorial services regarding the history, acquisition, identification or care of antique sundials and scientific instruments.*

SHATTERED PRODUCTIONS
P.O. Box 203
Aptos, CA 95001-0203
408 · 457 · 4277
♦ *Instructional booklet and video on the mosaic art of Piqué Assiette.*

From COPPER CRAFT LIGHTING, INC.

From CONSERVATOR'S EMPORIUM

PHOTO CREDITS

PHOTO EDITOR: Alexandra Truitt
PHOTO RESEARCH: Jerry Marshall

[l: *left*; r: *right*; m: *middle*; t: *top*; c: *center*; b: *bottom*]

COVER

© ALAN AND LINDA DETRICK.

POWER OF ORANMENT

Page 10 Jerry Harpur; *11* John Glover/Garden Picture Library; *12*t John Glover; *12*b Marie O'Hara/Garden Picture Library; *13*l Steven Wooster/Garden Picture Library; *13*tr Hugh Palmer; *13*br Ken Druse; *14*tl Ken Druse; *14*r Reinhard-Tierfoto; *15*l Derek Fell; *15*r Smith & Hawken; *16*tl Andrew Lawson; *16*bl Derek Fell; *16-17* Juliette Wade/Garden Picture Library; *17*tr John Glover/Garden Picture Library; *17*br JS Sira/Garden Picture Library; *18*l Howard Rice/Garden Picture Library; *18*r Nick Meers; *19*l Nick Meers; *19*r John Glover;

BORROWED FROM THE PAST

20 Vaughan Fleming/Garden Picture Library; *21* Steven Wooster/Garden Picture Library; *22*l Smith & Hawken; *22*r Howard Rice/Garden Picture Library; *23* Ping Amranand; *24*tl Richard Felber; *24*bl Richard Felber; *24*r John Bethel/Garden Picture Library; *25*l Derek Fell; *25*r John Glover; *26*tr Clive Nichols; *26*bl Brigitte Thomas/Garden Picture Library; *26*tr Karen Bussolini; *26*cr Jerry Pavia; *26*br Ald photo; *27*tl Hugh Palmer; *27*cl Jerry Pavia; *27*bl Ken Druse; *27*r Karen Bussolini; *28*t Jerry Pavia; *28*c Hugh Palmer; *28*b

Hugh Palmer; *29*tl Ald photo; *29*cl Richard Felber; *29*bl Derek Fell; *29*mt Ken Druse; *29*mc Harry Smith Horticultural Photographic Collection; *29*mb Marijke Heuff/Garden Picture Library; *29*tr Peter Jones; *29*cr Charles Mann; *29*br Juliette Wade/Garden Picture Library; *30*tl Ping Amranand; *30*bl Harry Smith Horticultural Photographic Collection; *31*tr Hugh Palmer; *31*br Ping Amranand; *32*l John Glover; *32*r Clive Boursnell/Garden Picture Library; *33*t Richard Felber; *33*tr Clive Nichols; *33*br Ron Evans/Garden Picture Library; *34*t Clive Nichols; *34*c Hugh Palmer; *34*b Jerry Pavia; *35*l Ted Hardin; *35*r Hugh Palmer; *36*l Smith & Hawken; *36*r Derek Fell; *37* Reinhard-Tierfoto; *38*tl Linda Joan Smith, Griggs Nursery; *38*bl Ken Druse; *38*r Reinhard-Tierfoto; *39*l Reinhard-Tierfoto; *39*r John Glover;

A SENSE OF PLACE

40 Charles Mann; *41* Charles Mann; *42*tl Charles Mann; *42*bl Tim Street-Porter; *42*r Nick Meers; *43*l John Glover; *43*tr Ping Amranand; *43*br Ping Amranand; *44*l Harry Smith Horticultural Photographic Collection; *44*r Charles Mann; *45*l Derek Fell; *45*tr Ken Druse; *45*br Charles Mann; *46*t Clive Nichols; *46*b Charles Mann; *47*t Derek Fell; *47*br Reinhard-Tierfoto; *47*bl Curtice Taylor; *48*t Gareth Rees Roberts/Pembridge Terracotta; *48*c

Linda Joan Smith, Griggs Nursery; *48*b Reinhard-Tierfoto; *49*t Charles Mann; *49*cl Derek Fell; *49*bl Richard Felber; *49*cr Charles Mann; *49*br Richard Felber; *50*t Brian Carter/Garden Picture Library; *50*b Vincente Motte; *51*l Steven Wooster/Garden Picture Library; *51*r Vaughan Fleming/Garden Picture Library; *52*tl JS Sira/Garden Picture Library; *52*bl JS Sira/Garden Picture Library; *52*r Ron Sutherland/Garden Picture Library; *53*l Harry Haralambou/Positive Images; *53*r John Glover; *54*t Clive Nichols; *54*b Jerry Pavia; *55*l Ping Amranand; *55*tr Dency Kane; *55*cr Jerry Harpur; *55*br Marijke Heuff/Garden Picture Library; *56*l Smith & Hawken; *56*r Derek Fell; *57*l Ping Amranand; *57*tr Hugh Palmer; *57*br Saxon Holt;

EYE CATCHERS AND SPACE MAKERS

58 Roger Hyam/Garden Picture Library; *59* Jerry Harpur; *60*l John Glover; *60*r Richard Felber; *61*tl Clive Nichols; *61*bl Smith & Hawken; *61*tr Ping Amranand; *61*cr Jerry Howard/Positive Images; *61*br Steven Wooster/Garden Picture Library; *62* Nick Meers; *63*l Andrew Lawson; *63*tr Jerry Harpur; *63*br Jonathan Buckley; *64*l Clive Nichols; *64*r Reinhard-Tierfoto; *65*l Clive Nichols; *65*tr Jerry Pavia; *65*br JS Sira/Garden Picture Library; *66*t Clive Nichols; *66*b Vincente Motte; *67*t

Clive Nichols; *67* bl Charles Mann; *67* br Ald photo; *68* l Clive Nichols; *68* tr Brigitte Thomas/Garden Picture Library; *68* cr Mick Hales; *68* br John Glover; *69* t Clive Nichols; *69* bl Clive Nichols; *69* br Dency Kane; *70* l John Glover; *70* r Ping Amranand; *71* t Clive Nichols; *71* b Ping Amranand; *72* l Clive Nichols; *72* tr Clive Nichols; *72* cr Clive Nichols; *72* br Jane Legate/Garden Picture Library; *73* t Charles Mann; *73* b Ping Amranand; *74* tl Jerry Harpur; *74* bl Ron Sutherland/Garden Picture Library; *74* br Charles Mann; *75* l Clive Nichols; *75* tr Dency Kane; *75* cr Charles Mann; *75* br Jerry Pavia;

WORKING ORNAMENT:

76 Clive Nichols; *77* Reinhard-Tierfoto; *78* l Harry Smith Horticultural Photographic Collection; *78* r Derek Fell; *79* l Richard Felber; *79* tr Clive Nichols; *79* br Derek Fell; *80* tl Clive Nichols; *80* bl Saxon Holt; *80* tr Jerry Pavia; *80* cr Linda Joan Smith, Pat Tillson; *80* br Karen Bussolini; *81* tl Richard Felber; *81* cl Sunniva Harte/Garden Picture Library; *81* bl John Glover; *81* ct Karen Bussolini; *81* tr Ken Druse; *81* cr Jerry Pavia; *81* br Jerry Pavia; *82* tl Gregory K. Scott, The National Audubon Society Collection/Photo Researchers; *82* bl Charles Mann; *82* r Richard Felber; *83* l Clive Nichols; *83* tr Lee Anne White/Positive Images; *83* cr Dency Kane; *83* br Ken Druse; *84* tl Saxon Holt; *84* bl Brian Carter/Garden Picture Library; *84* r John Glover; *85* l Neil Campbell-Sharp; *85* r Vincente Motte; *86* l Clive Nichols; *86* r John Glover/Garden Picture Library; *87* t Vincente Motte; *87* b Neil Campbell-Sharp; *88* t Clive Nichols; *88* b John Glover; *89* tl Harry Smith Horticultural Photographic Library; *89* cl John Glover; *89* bl Clive Nichols; *89* tr Harry Smith Horticultural Photographic Library; *89* cr Charles Mann; *89* br Charles Mann; *90* Richard Felber; *91* tl Clive Nichols; *91* bl Clive Nichols; *91* r Clive Nichols; *92* t Harry Smith Horticultural Photographic Collection; *92* b Charles Mann; *93* tl Charles Mann; *93* bl Charles Mann; *93* r Richard Felber;

OUT OF SEASON

94 John Glover; *95* Hugh Palmer; *96* tl Derek Fell; *96* bl Derek Fell; *96* r Harry Smith Horticultural Photographic Collection; *97* l Karen Bussolini; *97* r Clive Nichols; *98* tl Clive Nichols; *98* bl Harry Smith Horticultural Photographic Collection; *98* tr Harry Smith Horticultural Photographic Collection; *98* cr Hugh Palmer; *98* br Richard Felber; *100* t Charles Mann; *100* c Harry Smith Horticultural Photographic Collection; *100* b Charles Mann; *101* t Harry Smith Horticultural Photographic Collection; *101* b Harry Smith Horticultural Photographic Collection; *102* tl Jerry Harpur; *102* bl Charles Mann; *102* r Clive Nichols; *103* l Harry Smith Horticultural Photographic Collection; *103* tr Reinhard-Tierfoto; *103* br Jerry Harpur; *104* l John Glover/Garden Picture Library; *104* r Heather Angel; *105* l Karen Bussolini; *105* r Smith & Hawken; *106* Richard Brown; *107* t Richard Brown; *107* b Nick Meers;

LAYING CLAIM

Making the Garden Yours: *108* JS Sira/Garden Picture Library; *109* Charles Mann; *110* l Linda Joan Smith, Tor House; *110* r Charles Mann; *111* l Jerry Harpur; *111* tr Charles Mann; *111* br Charles Mann; *112* t Clive Nichols; *112* b Clive Nichols; *113* tl Linda Joan Smith, Ellen Fondiler; *113* cl Ping Amranand; *113* bl Harry Smith Horticultural Photographic Collection; *113* tr Linda Joan Smith, Ellen Fondiler; *113* cr Charles Mann; *113* br Clive Nichols; *114* tl John Glover; *114* bl Linda Joan Smith, Tor House; *114* r Charles Mann; *115* l Charles Mann; *115* r Smith & Hawken; *116* tl Clive Nichols; *116* bl Jerry Howard/Positive Images; *116* tr Reinhard-Tierfoto; *116* cr Derek Fell; *116* br Clive Nichols; *117* tl Richard Felber; *117* cl Reinhard-Tierfoto; *117* b Dency Kane; *117* tr Gary Rogers/Garden Picture Library; *117* cr Reinhard-Tierfoto; *118* l Charles Mann; *118* r Charles Mann; *119* l Charles Mann; *119* tr Charles Mann; *119* br Jerry Pavia; *120* l Smith & Hawken; *120* r Saxon Holt; *121* l Charles Mann; *121* r Jerry Pavia;

THE THINGS WE LOVE

122 Ken Druse; *123* Mel Watson/Garden Picture Library; *124* Harry Smith Horticultural Photographic Collection